Five
Audiences

Creative Leadership Series

Five
Audiences

Warren J. Hartman

Creative Leadership Series
Lyle E. Schaller, Editor

Abingdon Press/Nashville

Five Audiences

This book is printed on acid-free paper.

Library of Congress Cataloging-in-Publication Data

HARTMAN, WARREN J.
  Five audiences.
  (Creative leadership series)
  1. Pastoral theology. I. Title II. Series.
BV4011.H337   197   254'.5   86-14101

0-687-13052-2

The table "Qualities of Teachers Valued by Audience Groups," on p.
96, is from *A Study of the Church School in the United Methodist Church,* ©
1972 by the Board of Education of The United Methodist Church.
Used by permission.

MANUFACTURED BY THE PARTHENON PRESS AT
NASHVILLE, TENNESSEE, UNITED STATES OF AMERICA

To Mary Jane Crosley Hartman,
my wife and best friend

Foreword

For more than two centuries, many Protestant churches in America used gender as a primary means of dividing the congregation into smaller groups. A widespread example of that was the custom in many congregations for the women to sit on one side of the sanctuary and for the men to sit on the other side. A second was the use of gender in determining who was eligible for certain leadership positions.

An influential refinement of that pattern came in 1872 when a Chicago produce broker, B. F. Jacobs, persuaded the Sunday School Union to adopt the concept of a uniform lesson series that would be graded for different ages.

The 1930s brought high visibility to another system, as an increasing number of congregations began to organize classes and groups for married couples. Marital status was added to gender and age as focal points for organizing new groups. Tens of thousands of classes and groups were organized for married couples in the 1935–65 era. The use of marital status as a basic organizing principle flourished in the years after World War II, an era in which nearly all adults were married and most married relatively early in life. The use of marital status as a basic organizing principle continued in wide use in the 1960s, as some churches organized groups for single adults. The late 1970s brought the recognition that that was an overly simplistic approach to contemporary reality, and distinctive subgroups emerged under that umbrella label of "singles." Some were groups for formerly married, others were short-term experiences for people in the midst of a traumatic divorce, and an increasing number were for mature widowed women, while a relatively small number of churches began to organize groups for younger, never-married adults.

The 1970s also brought the concepts of stages of social development and stages of faith development. Those concepts were transformed into operational plans for building the group life of some churches.

Today a rapidly growing proportion of the adult population displays little interest in groups organized around the traditional focal points of age, gender, or marital status. The statistics on the decline in attendance since 1955 in adult Sunday school classes, or in participation in men's fellowships or women's organizations, document that disinterest. Today adults are more interested in joining groups that are organized in response to their needs. The tremendous growth in the parachurch Bible study groups for women represents one expression of that contemporary pattern.

In this book, Dr. Warren J. Hartman has pioneered a new approach to organizing the group life of the congregation. Instead of relying on gender, age, or marital status as the basic theme, Hartman has defined five "audiences," or subgroups. These are homogeneous groups based on beliefs, attitudes, expectations of the church, and other characteristics.

While the distribution of the members among these

five audiences will vary from one congregation to another, most churches will find that the overwhelming majority of the members will identify with one of these groups.

This classification may be the breakthrough congregational leaders have been seeking as they attempt to expand and reinforce the group life of their churches.

This volume is one in a series of books written for creative leaders who are seeking to enrich, reinforce, and expand the vitality and outreach of their churches. Dr. Hartman's contribution is an outstanding effort, as well as a lucid and readable analysis, for the benefit of those who seek to help more members find a meaningful place within a congregation's ministry.

Lyle E. Schaller
Yokefellow Institute
Richmond, Indiana

Contents

Preface

This is a book about people. They are just like the people you know in your congregation, or in your Sunday school class. When you meet the Bansons or the Eskins or Ruby Taylor, you will meet someone who reminds you of someone in your class or your congregation.

This book had its beginning in 1970. When we examined the responses of several hundred persons who were helping pre-test some questionnaires that had a number of open-ended questions, we noticed some definite patterns or configurations in the responses. If, for example, a respondent answered some questions in one way, he or she would also answer certain other questions in a predictable manner. Although the main purpose of that study was to gather other information, we decided to test a sub-hypothesis that there are distinct groups of persons in most congregations who can be identified by certain measurable characteristics.

Fourteen hundred lay persons, representing a nation-wide cross section of people, told us about themselves, what they believe, what they think others believe, and what they expect and want from their churches, their Sunday schools, their pastors, and their teachers and leaders.

When their responses were subjected to rigorous statistical analyses, five distinct groups of persons were identifiable. Each of these had a clearly different set of characteristics, attitudes, beliefs, and expectations. What is more, those in each group participated in the life of the church and Sunday school in a different manner.

We have called these groups *audience groups*. At times, we have referred to them simply as audiences or as groups. At other times we have referred to them by the descriptive labels or names we have given to them.

The labels that we have given to the audience groups may not be fully descriptive of those in each group. The names have been given for identification purposes and are not intended to be either descriptive or definitive of the groups.

The purpose of this book is to introduce the five audience groups, to describe them, and to suggest some of the implications for local church planning and programming.

This book has been in the process of evolution for more than fifteen years. The keen insights and perceptive observations of literally thousands of lay persons, professional colleagues, pastors, Christian educators, and church leaders are reflected in the pages that follow. To each of them we are deeply indebted and most grateful. They have offered comments and suggestions in numerous seminars, workshops, and leadership events in which the audience groups have been introduced. They have helped put flesh on the bony skeletons that were first sketched as each audience group began to take shape. They have also called attention to some of the changes that have been made and are still occurring among and within the different audience groups. Most importantly, they have repeatedly affirmed the presence of the different audience groups in their own congregations.

Persons who represent the five audience groups are found in all parts of the country and in every denomination where this concept has been introduced.

Our original study established the precise percentage of persons found in each audience group. We have not reported those percentages in these pages for two reasons. First, there is some evidence that recent national shifts in attitudes and beliefs are also operative in the church. As a consequence, the number of persons in some audience groups may be increasing, and in others the number may be decreasing. A second reason for not reporting the percentage distributions is that there may be some overriding denominational, regional, or local factors that could affect the number of persons found in each audience group. While the number of people in each audience group may shift from time to time and from place to place, the basic profiles of those in each group have remained relatively stable and constant.

One final word: Descriptions of the five audiences are based on statistical correlations that measure tendencies. They are by no means totally accurate, nor can human behavior be predicted with certainty. But this book is based on the evidence that when certain characteristics are present there is a strong possibility that certain other characteristics will be found also.

In the first chapter, we will introduce and give a brief descriptive overview of the five audience groups. Then

15

chapters 2 through 6 will each focus on one of the five groups. Each chapter will include one or more portraits of persons representing the audience group under consideration. The portraits will be followed by a discussion of the ways in which the dominant characteristics, beliefs, attitudes, expectations, and participation patterns find expression among those of each audience group. Each chapter will conclude with a list of implications for local church planning and programming.

Chapter 7 will point out some of the different expectations that those in each group have concerning their teacher or small group leader. Implications for grouping, leadership selection, class and group procedures, and curriculum needs will be identified and discussed.

In chapter 8 we have used a case study of a church to show how the ministry of one congregation was affected by the dominance of persons from two audience groups. Some strategies for helping the congregation develop a more comprehensive ministry will be suggested.

The final chapter will offer some suggestions and guidance to pastors and other leaders who want to assess the audience group distributions within their Sunday school classes, small groups, or entire congregation.

Now, let's meet our friends.

I

In the Same Congregation, but Different

"It's still raining," John Banson reported as he looked out the kitchen window for the tenth time. They had just finished their evening meal, and Marie, his wife, was just starting to clear away the dishes. She glanced over at John and replied, "Yes, and I'm glad that we don't have to go anywhere tonight. We can study our Sunday school lesson for tomorrow. You know, John, I never thought that I would lose interest in our Sunday school class, but I'm afraid I have."

John and Marie had helped organize the Home Builders' class about thirty-five years ago. It all started when they and three other newly married couples talked about having a class of their own. With the help of their pastor and the Sunday school superintendent, they organized the class, and the superintendent arranged for their curriculum resources. Everything went very well through the years, but now something was happening which John and Marie did not fully understand, nor did they know what they should try to do about it.

As they talked, they recalled some of the early developments in the class. "Do you remember," John asked with a note of excitement in his voice, "how we invited other young couples in the neighborhood to the class, and how we soon outgrew that first little classroom?"

"And how excited we were," Marie chimed in, "when they told us we could have the biggest classroom in the church if we would fix it up?"

John remembered that he was the class president at that time. Under his leadership, members of the class pitched in and redecorated the room. The men painted the walls and trim. The women made and installed curtains. They had several special projects to raise money for a used piano and a rug for the floor. They felt they had the finest classroom in the church.

Marie remembered with a chuckle that when she agreed to be the Sunshine Hostess, she planned to serve for only a year. But she had been re-elected so often that everyone now just assumed that she would continue indefinitely. She and John talked about the different couples who had come and gone through the years. They remembered the times of joy and celebration; the times of anxiety and sadness; the times of concern and pain; the times of disappointment and discouragement; the times of silly laughter and sheer happiness; and the times of victory and achievement. In a very real sense, the Home Builders' class was a large extended family within the church.

Through the years, as their children were growing up, different members of the class took turns teaching in the children's and youth Sunday school classes and in vacation Bible school. Some had served as counsellors for the youth fellowship. They had coached the ball teams, taken the kids on hayrides and weiner roasts, and supported them in their school activities.

Marie said, "I don't think I'll ever forget some of the

serious discussions we had about what we really believe, or some of our class parties, especially that time we all went out to George and Ruth's farm to sled on the big hill out in their pasture."

"Yes," John responded, "we've spent a lot of good times with those in our class. I wonder how many hours we have spent during the last thirty-five years talking and praying and laughing and, well, just being together."

But now things were changing. Jack Wilson had agreed about twenty years ago to serve as substitute teacher until a regular one could be named. Everyone liked Jack and his style of teaching so much that the class officers asked him to be their regular teacher. He agreed. His forceful and clear interpretations of the International Lessons rivaled many sermons. Sometimes the class got into some really interesting discussions. Other times the members were so caught up in Jack's presentations that no one wanted to interrupt him.

About six months ago Jack asked to be relieved of his teaching responsibilities due to health problems that he was having. The class officers asked their new pastor, the Reverend Bob Liberty, to fill in for a couple of weeks until they could recruit another regular teacher. He readily agreed and said that he enjoyed teaching so much that he would be glad to fill out the year. John and Marie, along with others, were pleased by that offer and told Bob so. Bob was an excellent Bible student, and he was deeply committed to Christ and the church. Everyone really liked him.

The first week or so, Bob taught in much the same style that Jack had used. Then, one Sunday he brought four different translations of the Bible to the class and pointed out the different way each had translated several verses that were at the heart of the lesson for that week. He raised several questions that no one could answer.

The next week, Bob announced that in preparation for the following Sunday he wanted everyone to watch their local paper for news articles dealing with faith and justice issues. They did not quite understand what he wanted, but some tried anyway. His favorite way of teaching was to raise questions and then divide the class into small groups to discuss the questions.

About a month ago, Bob had pointed out that since almost everyone went directly from the class into the worship service, they really did not need to spend quite as much class time in singing, announcements, prayer, and just talking about concerns and happenings related to members of the class. Such a change in procedure, Bob said, would give them more time for studying the lesson of the day. It sounded very logical, so members of the class agreed.

But things were not working out. Several couples stopped coming to Sunday school and had even missed the worship service the last two Sundays. One of John's best friends told him that he did not know if he would come back to the class again. He had been embarrassed when he did not know the answer to a question that someone had put to him in his small group. The easy banter and laughter that had always taken place before and after class sessions was missing. People did not seem to be quite so relaxed in the small groups as they had been in the larger group. Since they did not spend as much time for announcements and talking about some of their common concerns, they were beginning to feel that they were losing touch with one another.

John and Marie were bothered and puzzled. They felt something should be done, but they did not know what.

What was wrong? Nothing really, for some classes, that is.

Bob's method of teaching and conducting the class was very much in line with the way he had learned to teach while attending a lab school. But it was not working in the Home Builders' class. John and Marie and the others in the class had become accustomed to Jack's style of teaching and had become very comfortable with it. Now, Bob was introducing a different style of teaching which generated some entirely new dynamics in the class. In essence, he was attempting to restructure the class for people who were not there. The long-time members of the class did not know how to deal with their frustration.

They knew that Bob had taught another adult class, the Crusaders, for a few weeks during the Lenten season. The Crusaders had thoroughly appreciated his leadership. In fact, they had tried to persuade him to be their regular teacher, but he did not want to tie himself down to one class for a long period of time; so he declined.

Why would two adult classes in the same church have such different reactions to Bob's teaching? The classes were drawn largely from two of the five different audience groups that are found in most congregations Each audience group has characteristics and expectations that are unique to that group. Usually those in each group do not realize that they have expectations which are that different from those held by their friends in another audience group. But the differences do exist in several distinct areas.

First, persons in each audience group tend to have their own theological perceptions of themselves, of those in their class or group, of the majority of those in the congregation, of their pastor, and of their denomination.

Second, those in each audience group have certain identifiable personal and demographic characteristics. These include such things as age, gender, education, income, and, to a lesser degree, vocation or occupation, and the type of community or neighborhood in which they live.

Third, each audience group has its own set of attitudes and beliefs. They have distinct attitudes about social and moral issues, community and world affairs, and sometimes political matters. They may differ sharply in their beliefs. In the church and church school, those beliefs often include such things as biblical interpretation and translation; basic faith tenets concerning sin, salvation, the second coming, judgment, and the hereafter; and church polity and practice.

Fourth, closely related to their belief variances are the different ways those in each audience group participate in and relate to the church and the church school. These differences show up in attendance patterns, levels of denominational loyalty, and support for programs and projects. Differences are also noted in the level of their participation in religious groups and activities beyond the local church. In some instances, the differences are even seen in the leadership positions persons are most likely to hold in the local church.

John, Marie, the Home Builders' class, the Reverend Bob Liberty, and those in the Crusaders class all illustrate some of the different expectations that those in a particular audience group hold concerning their Sunday school class and teacher.

Representatives of each of the five audiences are very likely to be found in every congregation. Members of each group are just as apt to be found in a new surburban church as in Old First Church down on the city square. Representatives of each group are also just as likely to be found in a declining church as in a growing church. The only exception to this general rule is that sometimes the smallest membership churches may consist almost entirely of persons who exhibit the characteristics of one, or possibly two, audience groups.

In larger congregations, persons who are in the different audience groups tend to gather in separate Sunday school classes, women's groups, or other face-to-face primary groups. They are comfortable in those groups because they are associating with others who have similar interests and expectations. Even though the classes and groups may differ considerably from one another, congregations with larger member-ships can usually accommodate those differences without too much difficulty.

However, in many mid-size and most small member-ship congregations, there are normally not enough classes or small groups to provide a separate setting for each audience group. Consequently, the presence of representatives of several of the audience groups in the same Sunday school class or other small face-to-face group is often the source of more than a little tension and discomfort within the class or group.

As a result, there is a tendency for those in one audience group or the other to lose interest and possibly drop out altogether. The remaining audience group then becomes dominant in that class and the class takes on the characteristics of that audience group. When this self-selective process becomes operative in a majority of the classes and groups, the whole congregation may take on the characteristics of the dominant audience group or groups. Consequently, occasionally two congregations of the same denomination may be located within a few blocks of each other, but they may be quite different because each is dominated by a different set of audience groups.

Lest it be assumed that audience groups are static and permanently set, it should be noted that most persons pass through several audience groups at different times in their lives and at different stages of their faith journey. For example, although one of the dominant identifiers of the different audience groups is that of age, it cannot be assumed that just because a person is in a particular age group he or she will, therefore, exhibit all the characteristics of the audience group in which that age group is usually found.

Also, a number of complex and often interrelated factors may prompt persons to assume the characteristics of a different audience group. Some of the factors that often cause persons to move from one audience group to another are such things as changes in family or vocational status, certain personal or religious experiences, growing older, different responsibilities in the local congregation, or, perhaps, the strong influence of someone—a friend or relative, a church school teacher, or a pastor.

While the number of persons in each audience group may vary slightly in different regions of the country, the five audience groups are listed in the order of their size on a national scale, except for the last one, which is made up of several different combinations of the four other groups.

At this point, we will simply identify the five audience groups and give a very brief thumbnail sketch of some of their dominant general characteristics. Each of them will be examined in depth in the remaining chapters of this book.

Fellowship

The first audience group includes those whom we call the *fellowship group*. Persons in this group place a high value on interpersonal relationships. The level of their personal satisfaction and their church and church school participation is strongly affected by the kinds and the quality of their relationships with others in a class or other small group.

However, even though they thoroughly enjoy their association with others and want to have a good time with them, they are not fully satisfied with superficial relationships. They look for strong supportive relationships in which they can freely raise their questions, express their doubts, and share their faith. Since they depend largely on informal interpersonal relationships to satisfy their needs and expectations, they tend not to be overly concerned about or very interested in denominational or institutional relationships and concerns.

Traditionalists

The second audience group is made up of persons who are more *traditional* in their views and expectations than those in the other groups. They have a profound respect for and commitment to traditional customs, practices, values, and ways of doing things. This is especially true in respect to their religious faith and their church and church school.

They tend to be fiercely loyal to the local church, to their church school class, and to any other small groups to which they belong. And they do consider themselves to be belongers, and not merely attenders. They provide much of the stability in a congregation and maintain a strong link with its history and tradition. Because of their strong commitment to that which is and has been, they tend to have difficulty with changes that they feel are too frequent or too radical.

A recent phenomenon has been the emergence of an identifiable group of young adults who hold many characteristics in common with the older traditionalists; yet, they differ from them in several significant ways. We are therefore calling them *neo-traditionalists*. While the older traditionalists hold the denomination and their local congregation in high regard, the neo-traditionalists lodge their primary loyalty with the particular Sunday school class or small group to which they belong. The neo-traditionalists are also inclined to be more brittle and are often hostile toward those with whom they may differ.

Study

We have identified those in the third group as the *study group* because they are keenly interested in studying and learning about the Christian faith and life and the application of those understandings to their own lives and the world in which they live.

Their interests and concerns extend well beyond their class or small group to the congregation and beyond to the church at large. Their broad perspective of the faith and their commitment to its various expressions enable them to relate well to others, including those who may not always hold the same beliefs or views.

Persons in the study group are often in key leadership positions in their churches. Because of their progressive and broad views, they sometimes stimulate and lead the congregation in ways and directions that are misunderstood or not always appreciated by some members of the congregation.

Social Action

The fourth audience group is made up of those who have a deep concern about and commitment to the social dimensions of the Christian faith and life. They are strongly motivated to live out their faith as agents of social change. They want to participate in those dimensions of the church's ministry that address the problems and concerns of their community and world.

Their deeply felt concerns frequently take them well beyond their church school class and the congregation. Those in the *social action group* are inclined to view the class and other groups as launching pads from which they may move out into the midst of conditions and circumstances that they feel should be addressed.

Since those in the social action group are issue-oriented, they have little interest in the church or church school as organizational entities. Nor do they normally need a large support group. They are sometimes inclined to become impatient with others who do not share their intense concerns. Conversely, others tend to be turned off or even resentful of those whom they often look upon as being a bit too aggressive or too "far out."

Multiple Interest Group

The fifth group is a composite which includes persons whose characteristics are different combinations of the characteristics found in two or more of the four basic audience groups mentioned above. When the profiles of persons in the *multiple interest group* are compared with profiles of persons in the other four groups, the multiple interest characteristics fall at or very near the mid-point range in almost every instance. For example, the multiple interest persons perceive their theological position to be about halfway between that of persons in the traditional group and that of persons in the social action group. In that sense, we can say that those in the multiple interest group come quite close to a representation of the mythical "average layperson."

Another significant finding concerning the multiple interest group is that well over half of the persons tend to exhibit several of the dominant characteristics that are found in the fellowship group. For example, some multiple interest persons may exhibit a combination of fellowship and study group characteristics, or fellowship and traditional group characteristics. Others may have one or two dominant characteristics that are found among the fellowship group persons and several other dominant characteristics that are found in two or even all three of the other groups.

II

Friends Are Important

Bob Eskin was new in town. He had been sent by the home office to open a new territory for the rapidly growing line of computer software. His wife, Maxine, and their two children, Rob, seven, and Amy, three, were becoming old hands at this moving business. They had moved four times in the last nine years.

Saturday evening, while they were eating the fried chicken that Bob had picked up on the way home, Maxine asked, "Where shall we go to church tomorrow?"

"Oh, I don't know," Bob answered. "Why don't we try the church down the street?" Maxine agreed. So, the first Sunday they were in town they went to the nearest church.

They went in time for Sunday school because they wanted to meet some other young families, and they wanted Rob and Amy to get started right away in a Sunday school. Bob and Maxine had a little trouble finding classes for Rob and Amy, but they followed some other children into classes that seemed to be for about the same ages as their children. Bob and Maxine introduced Rob and Amy to the teachers and then began to look around for a young adult class. They found one, went in, and sat down. One couple spoke to them and gave them a study booklet. The teacher asked for their names, and just before beginning his lecture, he announced that the Eskins were visiting the class and invited them to come back again. When the bell rang, signaling the end of Sunday school, several persons nodded to Bob and Maxine as they rushed out the door. The teacher told them how glad he was to have them and expressed the hope they would come again.

Maxine went to the children's department and picked up Rob and Amy. Bob joined them, and they all went into the sanctuary for morning worship. The music was superb, and the pastor had a good sermon. After the benediction and the choral response, Bob and Maxine looked around. It seemed that everyone was too busy talking with someone else to notice them, so they made their way out of the church and to their car.

"I've had it with that church," Bob blurted out. "If they think I'm going back there again, they are badly mistaken," he continued.

"Yes, I feel the same way," Maxine replied. "Where do you want to go next Sunday, Rob?" She asked, turning to him.

"Can't we go back to our old church again?" begged Rob.

"I'm afraid that's not possible, but I promise you we'll find a Sunday school and church we will all like," replied his mother.

The next week when she was in the grocery store, Maxine overheard two women about her age talking about an upcoming Sunday school class party in another church in the neighborhood. It sounded like fun. Maxine introduced herself to them. She mentioned that she had overheard their conversation and told them that she and her family were new in town and were looking for a church with a friendly Sunday school for all members of the family.

"You have found it," exclaimed one of the women, who said her name was Doris. "Our Sunday school class is the best one in town. Why don't you and your husband plan to come to our class next Sunday, and we'll introduce you to some of the others in our class. Our party will be the next week and we'd like to have you come." They chatted a bit longer, then moved on toward the check-out.

Maxine could hardly wait for Bob to get home that evening. "I think I've found a church and a friendly Sunday school class," she said as she greeted him. Then she told him about the conversation she had in the grocery store.

"I've been thinking about that church last Sunday. Maybe it would be best just to wait a while," Bob replied. But Maxine insisted that, if for no other reason, they owed it to Rob and Amy to get them started right away in a good Sunday school. Bob reluctantly agreed.

When they arrived at the church on Sunday, Doris and her husband, Jack, met them at the door of the educational unit and greeted all four of the Eskins. Doris walked down the hall with them and introduced Rob and Amy to their teachers. Then Doris turned to Maxine and said, "Now, let's go to the class we were telling you about. I think you'll both like it." As they walked down the hall and neared the room where the class met, they heard someone laughing and several people talking. They stepped into the room, and Jack, who later turned out to be the class president, asked if they would like a cup of coffee. By the time the class was ready to begin, Bob and Maxine had met nearly everyone. Jack told about the grocery store conversation amid some good-natured banter from several members of the class and then welcomed Bob and Maxine before turning the class over to the teacher. There was a spirited discussion of several points in the lesson in which a number of the class took part.

When the class period was over, Maxine and Bob went by and got Rob and Amy, and they all went into the sanctuary for the morning worship service. The music in the worship service was not quite as outstanding as that in the other church, but the pastor made everyone feel welcome. Immediately after the benediction, a member of the Sunday school class came over and began to introduce the Eskins to those around them.

When they got to the car, Bob said excitedly. "I think we've found our church."

It was Rob who responded, "Yeah, since we can't go back to our old church, this will do just fine." Maxine and little Amy nodded in agreement.

Personal Demographics

Bob and Maxine are representative of many of those in the *fellowship audience group*. There is a higher percentage of men in this group than in any other audience group. The bulk of those in the fellowship group are found in two ages—young adults up to the middle or late thirties and those who are around fifty-five or older.

Many of the former are the drop-outs of the 1960s who have little or no church background. They want to find their way to a satisfying and fulfilling faith, but they are not sure what they want. They are reluctant to make binding commitments to a congregation, or even to a class, that would lock them into a permanent relationship. Yet, they know they want quality religious instruction for their children and most of them believe that the Sunday school is currently the best place to get it.

Those in the older age group are often persons whose last child has left home. Some of these older adults have moved to smaller homes that require less care. Many of them have been very involved in the activities of the church, the school, and the community, and now have decided they want to give up some of their leadership responsibilities. But they still enjoy the fellowship of friends and associates.

Vocationally, a high percentage of those in the fellowship group are in occupations or are following careers that require them to move frequently from place to place. Others are on the road much of the time. Military personnel, salespersons, persons in middle management, and those in similar positions make up a large portion of the group.

Educationally, they report the third highest level of achievement. Yet, they report the highest average level of income. Normally, income is correlated with educational attainment, but the large number of men in this group and the presence of vocational careers that are often associated with above average incomes may be offsetting factors.

Theological and Belief Patterns

Theologically, those in the fellowship group range all the way from the very conservative to the very liberal. In fact, they are not inclined to place much emphasis on their theological perspective; many really don't know or don't care. When pressed for an answer, they are most likely to view themselves almost precisely at the same point on the theological continuum that they place their pastor, or the majority of those persons in the small group or class to which they belong.

The fact that they are not particularly articulate about their faith should not be interpreted to mean that they are not interested in faith issues. Some of them have developed a very strong faith, and spiritual disciplines are very much a part of their daily life. Others are still searching. For most of those in the fellowship audience group, the kind of faith that really matters is expressed in day-to-day relationships.

Generally, those in the fellowship group do not attach much importance to denominational labels. They have belonged to more denominations than those in any other group. The theological position of a local church or the denominational label is not a major consideration when they are choosing a new church home. Nor do most of them attach much importance to the tradition and history of a particular local congregation or of a denomination. They want to know what a church and its people are like today. They are not overly impressed by what it has been or what it might become in the future.

Their primary interest is in the quality of congregational life and the kind of interpersonal relationships that are offered. To them, those very real and personal experiences are much more important than the theological climate, the way in which the Bible is interpreted, or the manner in which the church is organized to carry on its ministry.

Church and Sunday School Participation

Those in the fellowship group are not among the most regular or frequent attendees of worship services. In fact, they have one of the poorest records of worship attendance, except in the smallest congregations where they can know and associate with everyone. Their poor attendance is not due to any hostility or dislike for the pastor. On the contrary, they are often very friendly toward the pastor. They simply do not feel a need for the larger congregational relationships and experiences. Nor do they feel a strong sense of loyalty and commitment to the congregation as a whole. They tend to lodge their loyalties with those primary groups that foster face-to-face relationships. For that reason, it is exceedingly important for large congregations to offer a number of Sunday school classes and other small groups to those who are in the fellowship group.

While they maintain the third highest record of attendance in the formal class sessions of the Sunday school, their record of attendance and level of participation in informal gatherings and other settings that offer opportunities for fellowship is very high. They readily join and enthusiastically participate in athletic events, week-end activities, neighborhood groups, and Sunday school class parties and other social or fellowship events.

Those in the fellowship group are not inclined to accept many leadership responsibilities outside the primary group to which they belong. They will, however, accept leadership in the groups mentioned above and in some activities involving children and youth. They are often found coaching the church

35

softball team, serving as leaders in the Scout troop, directing work camps, taking groups on camping trips or tours, and occasionally, serving as counsellors for the evening youth fellowship. They show much less interest in formal organizational and administrative matters. Informality and only the barest essentials of formal structures are to their liking.

They look to the church, the Sunday school classes, the men's fellowship, and the women's groups as places where they can find ready acceptance and a supportive group of friends. They are not looking for superficial relationships. They can, and do, establish new and deep friendships quickly. Conversely, some of them, especially the young adults without children, are able to sever relationships and move on to new fellowship groups relatively easily. If the group to which they belong ceases to satisfy their need for deep and meaningful relationships, they may not stay around; rather, they will look elsewhere. They may look to another church or to another group in the congregation.

Those in the fellowship group who have dropped out of the church say the primary reason was a feeling that they were not wanted or did not belong. If they do return, they will most likely say that they were influenced to do so by a teacher or some of their friends.

Specifically, what are the things they look for and expect to find in their Sunday school classes and other small groups? Those in the fellowship audience group want to belong to classes and small face-to-face groups that function in an informal manner and on a first name basis. They want time for chatting informally with one another before and after the formal class session. A coffee pot and some kind of refreshment are often standard equipment in groups that are made up of those who are fellowship-oriented.

They appreciate opportunities to share with others in their joys and concerns, to celebrate birthdays and anniversaries, to recognize achievements, promotions, and job changes, and to support and pray for the members of their group when illness or misfortune strikes.

They prefer teachers and leaders who encourage discussion. They are comfortable in relatively large classes, providing there is ample time and space for informal fellowship and discussion. In larger groups, they sometimes appreciate opportunities to break up into smaller discussion groups of five or six. They are not particularly concerned about what kind of curriculum is used, providing it is relevant and has meaning for them now. They want ample opportunities to raise their questions, to share their faith experiences, and to express their doubts and concerns—all in an informal and supportive environment.

Those in the fellowship group expect some of the relationships to extend through the week. These may include such things as getting together with another family or two from the class for a cook-out, a night at the bowling alley, an afternoon or evening of bridge, a home Bible study group, caring for one another's children, or taking in a meal when someone is ill.

What Are the Implications?

1. Remember that those in the fellowship group are primarily interested in the quality of personal relation-

ships that a congregation can provide for them and their friends now. Those relationships override every other factor, without exception. Someone put it this way, "I want to find my kind of people and when I have found them, I have found my church."

2. Since they include many young adults, efforts should be made to form new groups as they are needed. The groups should be designed to meet their expectations. Young adults, especially, are very reluctant to move into a group that has been in existence for some time, or one that has reached its optimum size.

3. Careful thought should be given to the selection of the teacher or leader. He or she should encourage the development of personal relationships in the group and should be able to function in a flexible, yet consistent, manner.

4. Rapid assimilation is important, especially for the newcomers. They tend to be impatient in their eagerness to learn to know others and to be accepted into a group. One young mother said, "We may not live here very long and our family needs a place where we can put down some roots now."

5. Try to guard against enlisting them for leadership responsibilities before they are ready or when they are reluctant to do so. Likewise, efforts to lead them to faith commitments may require much patience and careful guidance.

6. Remember that many in this group do not cherish the denominational heritage or traditions in the same way that others do. They tend to be very contemporary, and many of them have little appreciation for the things and people of the past. So, an appeal to them on the

basis of past denominational ties usually has no effect.

7. Since those in the fellowship audience group have strong needs for fellowship, they want ample space and time to move around in the room. They usually do not attach much importance to a particular room, so they are comfortable in a relatively large fellowship hall with chairs set up in a circle or semi-circle.

8. Arrangements should be made for a number of social events for all classes that include fellowship-type persons. Any number of different social activities can be planned. The kinds of programs and types of entertainment are not nearly so important as opportunities for the class just to be together.

9. Select teachers and class officers who are gregarious and extroverted. Try to keep the same teacher or class officers for fairly long tenures in order to provide some continuity and stability.

10. If you expect the fellowship classes to include single adults, do not call them "couples" classes or plan social events that exclude single adults.

11. Since a growing number of adults do not drink caffeinated coffee, be sure to offer a choice of beverages. Tea, decaffeinated coffee, or fruit juice are good alternatives.

12. A class host or hostess, or a "Sunshine" person will help first-time visitors get acquainted and can keep the class informed about birthdays, anniversaries, illness, address changes, and other personal information that is very important to those of the fellowship audience.

13. Since those who are in the fellowship group place a high value on relationships with those in a class or small group, a call or visit from another member of the

class or group often means more to them than a visit from the pastor.

14. Fellowship group persons often appreciate the use of different kinds of media, such as film clips, slides, video cassettes, guest speakers, panel discussions, outside speakers, and others.

III

Beliefs Do Matter

The wind had been blowing across the wheat fields for three days without any sign of letting up. "If this keeps up, we'll start harvesting week after next," Ralph Orton remarked to his wife, Sally. "I wonder if Ed and I can get a couple of others to help us put the new roof on the church before then." The roof had been damaged when a freak hail storm cut a narrow swath through the area a few weeks earlier. At first, Ralph and Ed thought they could wait until after harvest to repair it, but the roof had leaked in several spots during the hard rain last week. So they decided that they should make the repairs before they started harvesting.

The church had always occupied a big place in their lives. In fact, Sally had never belonged to another church. Her parents were among those who had helped organize the church. When Sally and Ralph were married they rented a farm in the community at first, then bought it. Then Ralph and their son Jim also took over the homeplace when farming became too difficult for Sally's father. Jim had completed a degree in agriculture at the state college and really appreciated the opportunity to introduce the latest technology into the enlarged farm operation. Jim's brother and sister also graduated from the state college, with degrees in electrical engineering and computer science. They have good positions in nearby cities and still like to come back to the home church when they can.

For Ralph and Sally the church is where they meet many of their neighbors every week. Since their pastor serves another church in the county seat and does not live in their community, they have taken it upon themselves through the years to make many of the decisions concerning the church and its program in the absence of their pastor. For example, they decided that they still liked the King James version of the Bible, so they always read the Sunday school lesson from it in the opening exercise of the Sunday school; Ralph and Ed have taken their turns serving as the Sunday school superintendent.

Ed's father has taught the adult Sunday school class as long as anyone can remember. He can always be counted on for an excellent lesson. Sally says that he is "the best read Bible student" she has ever heard. There are no surprises in the way the class is conducted. They begin with a prayer, then report any news about one another, those who are sick, and perhaps give an explanation why someone is absent. Then Ed's father teaches the lesson. They have always used the International Lesson Series, because they like the strong emphasis on Bible study. Sometimes there is a good discussion in response to the teacher's question, but they usually prefer to listen. They often close the Sunday school class session by praying the Mizpah benediction, "May the Lord watch between me and thee while we are absent one from the other."

Ralph and Sally really love their church and the people in it. Most of them have been worshiping together, studying the Bible in Sunday school together, and caring for one another for a long time. They have become like one big family.

Judy Owens is an architect. As a child and youth, Judy was very active in her local church, along with the other members of the Owens family. When she moved from the Midwest to a school on the West Coast to prepare for her career, she went to a church for a couple of weeks. Then she became so involved with her studies that she stopped going, except on special occasions.

One day a student who sat next to her in the lecture hall, Linda, told her about a weekend retreat that was being planned by a nondenominational campus group. Suddenly, Linda said, "I have an idea. Why don't you come along? We have reserved a lodge in the state park and have plenty of room. We plan to take the hiking trail, do some horseback riding, and we'll have an old-fashioned songfest around the fireplace at night."

"It sounds like fun," Judy replied. "It makes me think of the weekend trips our youth fellowship back home used to take. I'll think it over." During the week Judy kept thinking about Linda's invitation and her excitement as she described the weekend. Finally, Judy made up her mind and told Linda that she'd go with her.

The weekend was everything that Judy had hoped it would be, and more. She realized that she had been missing the kind of fellowship that she used to enjoy with the old gang at home. Most of all, she realized that she had missed the church and those interesting discussions about the Christian faith. After the retreat, she began to attend the Bible study that was led by one of the fellows who had led a discussion during the retreat.

Judy became deeply interested in the Bible study sessions and in the other activities of the campus fellowship group. One summer she decided to join several others from the group in a witness mission to Japan. Each of them raised his or her own money for expenses. By the time she completed her senior year, Judy was planning and leading weekend retreats, and she had organized a Bible study group that met every week.

When Judy graduated from the university, an architectural firm in Texas offered her an excellent position. After prayerfully considering the offer and talking with some of her good friends in the campus fellowship, she decided that it was God's will that she should accept the position.

As soon as she found an apartment and had started to work, she began to look for a church which provided the opportunities for Bible study and spiritual growth that she had known in the campus fellowship group. She visited several churches, and although none of them came up to her highest expectations, one of them had a Sunday school class for young adults that emphasized Bible study. They called themselves the Bible Fellowship class.

Judy joined that class and was soon deeply immersed in its life and activities. Not only did they study directly from the Bible, but they also used books on prophecy, and a number of the class members subscribed to a magazine that told about some of the ways that biblical prophecy was being fulfilled each year.

When some other members of the congregation questioned this class about the curriculum being used, the members of the Bible Fellowship class were surprised. They truly felt that the members of their class were growing in their faith and did not believe that those who chose to belong to other classes had a right to question their choice of curriculum resources or the subjects they studied.

Nevertheless, those who belonged to the Bible Fellowship class were determined to continue studying the Bible in much the same manner that they had been, because it had been a real source of spiritual growth and understanding. "After all," Judy commented, "that's what the Christian faith is all about."

Personal Demographics

Ralph and Sally Orton and the Bansons, whom we met in the first chapter, both exhibit some of the dominant characteristics that are usually found in the traditional audience group. Judy Owens is a representative of the neo-traditionalists. While the traditionalists and neo-traditionalists hold many charcteristics in common, they each have distinctive characteristics that set them apart. In the paragraphs which follow, we will discuss the traditionalists first, then follow with a discussion of the neo-traditionalists.

John and Marie Banson are representative of those traditionalists who are associated with larger congregations. For them, the Home Builders' Sunday school class has become a small congregation that has a life of its own within the larger congregation.

Ralph and Sally Orton are typical of the traditionalists who belong to smaller rural congregations in which the traditionalists constitute the majority of those in the church. Through the years, especially as many of the younger members have moved away, the traditional pattern has become the norm for the congregation. Those who are inclined toward the characteristics of one of the other groups have either lost interest and have dropped out, have transferred to another church, or have adopted some of the traditional ways and have become comfortable with them.

The majority of the traditionalists, like the Bansons and the Ortons, are among the older members of the church. They tend to have completed less formal education than those in any other group, and they report the lowest level of income as a group. Vocationally, many are blue collar workers or farmers.

There is, however, a sizable minority among the traditionalists who have above average education and income. They are often bankers, administrators, business executives, or owners of businesses. They also help to maintain the traditional values, not only in the church, but also in the community.

Theological and Belief Patterns

Most traditionalists suscribe to a theological position that is definitely to the right of center. In the mid-size and larger congregations, most of the traditionalists are inclined to believe that others in the congregation hold to theological positions that tend to be quite liberal. But in the smaller congregations, the traditionalists are not so inclined to feel that others in the congregation are any more liberal than they are.

The majority of traditionalists, regardless of the size of their congregation, feel that their pastor holds to a theological position that is much more liberal than the one to which they adhere. Most of them also feel that there is a wide gap between their views and those of their denomination.

Because of this perception, many traditionalists find support for their position in some of the radio and television personalities to whom they listen regularly. This is especially true for those who attend the smaller rural churches that are served by part-time or nonresident pastors. When such is the case, the traditionalists are not sure whose position is right for them. Their regular and frequent exposure to the very effective communicators who come into their homes via the air waves often generates a level of trust and familiarity that is greater than that which is granted to the local pastor. When the biblical interpretations and theological positions of the pastor are perceived to be different from their own and those of their favorite radio or television personality, traditionalists are troubled indeed.

Church and Sunday School Participation

Traditionalists maintain the highest record of attendance in the worship services of their church. Despite any theological differences they might have with the pastor or others in the congregation, they are fiercely loyal to their local church. Furthermore, they will drive farther in order to participate in the services of the church than will those in any other group. This is especially true if the church has a cemetery, or if there is some kind of memorial dedicated to a family member. They believe worship service attendance is important, they cherish their heritage, and they are faithful to their commitment to others in the congregation and to the church.

Traditionalists have been members of their congregations longer than those in any other group. A higher percentage of them have also belonged to the same denomination for the longest period of time. It is very difficult for them to change local congregations, and it is even more difficult to switch denominations when that becomes necessary due to a move to a new community or to some other circumstance.

They attach much importance to continuity and order. They may not be formally organized, but their manner of doing things is consistent and predictable.

They believe very strongly that their congregation should be engaged in a program of evangelistic outreach. The traditionalists will give considerable time and effort to supporting such efforts. Most of them are deeply committed to denominational mission and outreach efforts, but many also believe that they are justified in withholding their money if they do not feel the church is spending it wisely or for the right causes.

As a group, traditionalists have little confidence in most expressions of the consiliar movement or most interdenominational expressions, particularly on a national or world scale. They are inclined to suspect such movements. Some think that the ecumenical movements are soft on Communism and weak in their support of democracy and the American dream.

Generally, because of their high sense of commitment to the church, traditionalists are not inclined to drop out of the church easily. But if they should drop out for one reason or another, the pastor, some of those in their Sunday school class, or a trusted friend who shares their views and concerns would be most influential in their decision to return.

Those in the traditional audience group maintain the second highest record of Sunday school attendance. They like a Sunday school class that follows a consistent routine from Sunday to Sunday. Opening and closing procedures vary with the size of the class and the physical facilities. They usually include some time for prayer and perhaps devotional thoughts. Time is spent acknowledging the presence of any visitors or members of the class who have returned after an illness, vacation, or absence of several weeks. They make reports concerning those who are ill or unable to be present. Often those who will be absent will inform a member of the class beforehand and that will be reported to the class. Perhaps references will be made to the illness of others in the community who may not be members of the congregation, but are well known by all. Occasionally, a special offering is taken on the spot, or a plan of action is set in motion to meet a need of someone in the congregation or community. If the class and room are large enough, the class may have a piano and they may sing a gospel hymn or two every week.

Just as they usually follow a fairly consistent pattern for beginning the class period, so they often have a traditional way of concluding the class period. In some classes, the class president or someone other than the teacher may offer a spoken prayer or may lead the class in praying a unison prayer or benediction.

Traditionalists want a teacher who is biblically oriented and who gives evidence of his or her own personal faith. Even though they may not always agree with the teacher, they do expect the teacher to have strong convictions about what he or she believes, and they expect the teacher to express those beliefs. They expect their teacher to have some authority based on personal experience, knowledge of the Bible, and acquaintance with Christian beliefs.

Most traditionalists prefer the International Lesson Series or similar curriculum resources which are definitely biblically oriented. The older traditionalists may prefer to use the King James Version of the Bible either exclusively or as a normative point of reference and comparison to other translations. Generally, they prefer to stick with a series Sunday after Sunday and are reluctant to interrupt the lesson in order to join with another class for a special occasion or program.

They prefer a teacher who lectures. It is not uncommon for the same teacher to lead the same class for a number of years without interruption. When this happens, the class may be known informally by the name of the teacher, such as "Mr. Edgar's class," rather than by some other title.

Although traditionalists enjoy being together for the class sessions, they usually do not attach much importance to monthly class parties or social activities. They may have an occasional "get-together" during the holidays, but they do not, as a rule, feel the need for many social events and activities apart from the regular Sunday class sessions.

Because they tend to prefer a teacher who lectures, the Sunday school class may be quite large in some churches. In those cases, the class officers have an important role and may be elected on an annual basis. In other classes which are smaller, administrative functions, such as record keeping and taking up the offering, might be taken care of by the teacher or someone who has functioned in that capacity for some time.

The Neo-traditionalists

Now, let's look at the *neo-traditionalists*. As previously implied, neo-traditionalists have emerged in fairly large numbers during the last fifteen or twenty years. They share many theological views, a commitment to the centrality of the Holy Scriptures, and the belief in the importance of an experiential faith with the traditionalists. But neo-traditionalists have different expectations concerning the church and Sunday school, and their participation patterns may be different from those of the traditionalists.

Many of the neo-traditionlists, like Judy Owens, are coming back into the life of a denominationally associated church after previous involvement in one or more of the quasi-denominational groups. Others may have been strongly influenced by some of the electronic age religionists. Still others, perhaps because they dropped out of the church in the sixties and early seventies are aware of a deep unmet spiritual need, and they are looking for a biblical and theological mentor to assist in their faith pilgrimage.

As a group, neo-traditionalists tend to have more formal education than do traditionalists. Some neo-traditionalists are blue collar workers. Others have highly skilled, highly technical careers. There are also significant numbers of neo-traditionalists who have above average formal education, and, like Judy Owens, are pursuing professional careers. In fact, neo-traditionalists are to be found in almost every occupation.

Like traditionalists, neo-traditionalists perceive their theological position to be to the right of center. They also consider the majority of those in the congregation, the denomination, and most local church pastors to be considerably more liberal than are they.

Neo-traditionalists are not quite so inclined to come under the influence of electronic evangelists as are traditionalists. But they do tend to be more responsive to some of the quasi-religious groups and their leaders with whom they are personally acquainted. Some neo-traditionalists are also strongly influenced by the books and magazines that they read.

Neo-traditionalists and Their Sunday School and Church

Neo-traditionalists are inclined to lodge their primary loyalty in the Sunday school or small group to which they are related and their secondary loyalty in the congregation and denomination. Consequently, they usually maintain a high record of attendance in their Sunday school class and other small groups, but may not be so regular in the larger groups, such as worship services. In fact, some neo-traditionalists may not attend the worship services at all, especially if they are at odds with someone in the congregation or with the pastor.

Neo-traditionalists usually do not attach as much importance to the tradition of the congregation or to its denominational relationships as do traditionalists. It is not unusual in some communities for neo-traditionalists to switch easily from one church to another in their search for a Sunday school class or Bible study group that best satisfies their needs.

Neo-traditionalists' Expectations and Preferences

As a general rule, neo-traditionalists are not bound to a single translation of the Bible, but may use several of the newer and contemporary versions. Nor do they always prefer the International Lesson Series. The primary requirement is that the curriculum resources must be strongly Bible-oriented as opposed to issue-oriented. If they do use issue-oriented resources, the subjects are often related to spiritual formation, doctrinal issues, personal witnessing, biblical prophecy, and Christian family life.

The neo-traditionalists tend to prefer a Sunday school class that welcomes discussion along with lecture. They want a teacher who is a good Bible student and has strong convictions which grow out of an experiential faith. They want a teacher with whom they can talk and sometimes debate.

They often have a coffee pot and some kind of refreshment in their classroom. They do not attach much importance to their classroom or place of meeting. They like and will participate in a number of social activities in addition to the study class sessions. Neo-traditionalists are very appreciative of social activities that include noticeable spiritual dimensions, such as a concluding period of worship or a brief devotional thought for the day.

Relationships with Others

One notable difference between the older traditionalists and the younger neo-traditionalists is their attitude toward those who are theologically at variance with them. Traditionalists are usually not hostile, but do evidence deep concern and sometimes frustration and confusion. Neo-traditionalists, on the other hand, are inclined to look on those who are at variance with them as being their adversaries. They are often openly hostile toward others and are very defensive of their beliefs and those whose views they espouse.

Some Common Characteristics

Both the traditionalists and neo-traditionalists find support for their positions in some of the popular books on prophecy and religion and in their association with like-minded persons in the church, at work, in neighborhood groups, and in community-wide groups that are often inter- or nondenominational.

Traditionalists and neo-traditionalists both take their beliefs very seriously. When compared with those in the other audience groups, a much higher percentage of those in this group (especially the traditionalists) say they have been born again and have accepted Jesus Christ as their personal Savior and Lord. They feel very strongly about the central importance of the Holy Scriptures and the regular exercise of spiritual disciplines. They believe that the primary purpose of the church should be clearly identified with spiritual matters. Since their beliefs are of supreme importance, it is most distressing to them when others differ about matters of faith and belief.

What Are the Implications?

1. The deep commitment that traditionalists and neo-traditionalists have to a personal relationship with Jesus Christ as their Savior and Lord can add a significant quality to the life and witness of every congregation.

2. The importance that traditionalists and neo-traditionalists attach to biblical study and to doctrinal beliefs

serves as a reminder of that which is central to the Christian faith and life.

3. While the traditionalists and neo-traditionalists tend to hold similar beliefs and share a common interest in Bible study, they may have different expectations concerning Sunday school class procedures, the style of the teacher, curriculum resources, and classroom arrangements and facilities.

4. The desires and expectations of those in this audience group concerning curriculum resources and the manner in which they are taught should be honored and respected. To insist that they use different curriculum resources or that they engage in a discussion when they prefer a lecture is to do them a disservice, and it may generate unnecessary tension.

5. When teachers or leaders are needed for traditional or neo-traditional classes, attention should be given to the selection of persons who are strongly Bible-oriented, can articulate the meaning of their own personal faith, and who can and will teach in a manner and style that satisfies the expectations of those in the class.

6. Pastors should be aware of the confusion and conflict that may be generated by the very real and honest differences in theological perceptions and biblical interpretations that often exist between those in this audience group and the other members of the congregation and/or the pastor.

7. The fierce loyalty that traditionalists have for the local church provides continuity and a very valuable sense of history and tradition.

8. It is important to recognize the significance that traditionalists attach to a classroom or a place they can call their own. When the classes are large, they may want a piano, a lectern, a sound system, and other aids.

9. Because it is often difficult for newcomers to break into a traditional class or group that has a long history, local congregations would do well to organize new classes that are specifically designed for both traditionalists and neo-traditionalists.

10. Many traditionalists express their faith and their creativity through their hands or some physical expression rather than through verbal skills; therefore, they do not like to be put on the spot with questions or assignments that require an articulated response.

11. Because traditionalists are strongly mission oriented, their tie with the denomination may be strengthened by arranging for direct financial support for a missionary they have met.

12. Neo-traditionalists may offer a new challenge and opportunity to the mainline denominations. Many of them can serve as bridges to the thousands of other young adults who are seriously searching for a congregation that will provide nurture and a climate for their faith development.

13. Since many neo-traditionalists have little denominational background or may have been associated with a wide variety of religious groups, it is important to assign teachers and leaders who are well informed about denominational polity and beliefs.

14. The tendency of many neo-traditionalists to anchor their primary loyalty in a class or small group, rather than in the life of the congregation or of a denomination, underscores the fragile relationship that many of them have with the larger community of believers. This calls for concerted efforts on the part of the pastor and the congregational leaders to discover ways to assimilate them into the life of the total congregation.

IV

A Growing Faith

Ben and Susan Radcliffe came to town several years ago when Ben was hired as the new school superintendent. Susan is a registered nurse who specializes in geriatric care. Their daughter, Marie, is now a senior in high school.

As long as they can remember, their Christian faith has always been an important part of their lives. They have always been deeply involved in the life of the church and in its various ministries, both locally and in the wider expressions of ministry. Since the church is a very important part of their lives, they spent several hours when they first moved to town in talking about where they would place their church membership.

Ben said he hoped to find a Sunday school class or some other small group where they could really dig into the meaning of the gospel for today's world. Sally agreed, but said: "I think I really need to be challenged and inspired through the worship services. Although I would not consider any other work, I must admit that there are times when my work gets to me, and I need to be charged up for the coming week." Marie, who was a sixth grader at the time, piped up with, "Don't forget that I want to find a church that has a lot of good things for kids, too!" They continued to think of the church they hoped to find and came up with several additional characteristics, including the friendliness of the people and an openness to new ideas.

In summary, they agreed that they were looking for a church that had a strong educational program, including a well rounded program for children and youth. They expected the worship services to be inspiring and challenging. They were interested in opportunities for fellowship and service, both within the congregation and with persons from other churches. They wanted to find a church that cooperated with other churches in the community, yet also had a strong sense of identity with the denomination. It must be one in which they would feel at home. Above all, the church they would choose must be one in which they would each grow in an understanding of and a commitment to the Christian faith and life.

So, after inquiring around and visiting several congregations, they decided to place their membership in Faith Church. During the time that they have been a part of this congregation, each member of the Radcliffe family has been actively involved in the church. Susan has sung in the choir and has found real support in the women's mission study group that meets on Tuesday evenings.

Marie enrolled in the confirmation class the first year that they were in the church. Recently, she has been caught up in a swirl of youth activities—Sunday school, summer work camps, weekend retreats, and youth choir. Right now, she is the president of the youth fellowship and has been named to represent the district in a state youth convocation.

Ben found just the Sunday school class for which he had been looking. It is made up of several couples who are about the same age and who have common interests. Susan isn't always as excited about the class discussions as Ben is, but she thoroughly enjoys the close-knit fellowship of those in the class. Two other couples from the class have become Ben and Susan's best friends; they have a tradition of getting together whenever one of them has a birthday or one of the couples celebrates their anniversary.

Ben has taken his turn teaching the class, has served as the chairman of the official governing board of the church, and through the years has chaired several important committees and task forces in the congregation. He was especially pleased to represent the congregation in the annual legislative and planning body for the state, and has been named to represent the churches of his area in two national conferences. Faith Church has surely been everything the Radcliffes had hoped for when they selected it as their church home.

Jack Graham was just out of law school. He had been reared in a rural community where he had been a leader in the 4-H Club, had represented his local church in several district and state conferences, and had been a three star athlete in high school. He graduated summa cum laude from college and did postgraduate work in law. Now, he has an excellent opportunity with a legal firm in the state capital. The position has an extra appeal for Jack because he hopes to try his hand in politics someday, and being in the state capital will enable him to observe the legislators and to become personally acquainted with some of them.

But there was something missing in his life. While in school, Jack was so busy holding down a part-time job while carrying a full academic load that he had not bothered to attend church very often. Shortly after he had taken the job with the law firm, one of his associates, Ralph Gordon, whom he had enjoyed learning to know, asked Jack if he had found a church yet. Jack was a bit taken aback and made some lame excuse. His mother had asked him the same question the last time he was home. The little rural church had always occupied an important place in his family when Jack was growing up. He suddenly realized that he was missing the kind of close fellowship and inspiration that he used to know in that little church back home.

Jack began to attend the worship services in several churches, but nothing was really attractive to him. Then he decided to ask Ralph about the church he and his family attended. Ralph said, "Better yet, why don't you come and go with us, and then come have Sunday dinner with us. I've been telling Joyce about you, and I want you to meet her and the kids."

Jack met Ralph at the church. Joyce soon joined them after taking little Beth to her Sunday school class. Then they went to their Sunday school class. Ralph introduced Jack to several others who had gathered around to drink coffee and have a doughnut. The class was made up of other young professionals, both single and married. Their teacher, who was a bit older than the others, introduced the subject for the day, then skillfully engaged the members in a rather intense discussion. Jack found himself getting involved, and before he knew it he was vigorously advocating an idea that he felt quite strongly about.

Jack accompanied Ralph and Joyce to the worship service. He had visited the same congregation several weeks ago, and although the sermon was an excellent one and the choir was equally as good, he did not see anyone he knew and he left immediately. This time it was different. Ralph and Joyce introduced Jack to several others who sat near them. Then Ralph introduced Jack to the minister, who warmly welcomed him and told him about several other activities that he thought would be of interest to him.

Jack returned the next Sunday and the next. He felt good about going to church again. In a couple of weeks, the pastor called on Jack. When he learned of Jack's background in the little rural church, his strong convictions, and his inquisitive mind, he asked Jack if he would serve as a small group discussion leader in an upcoming retreat they were planning for the college class. Jack hesistantly agreed, but down inside himself he knew that he had found a church home.

Personal Demographics

Ben Radcliffe and Jack Graham are among those whom we have called the *study group*. Susan Radcliffe also exhibits some of the characteristics, but has other interests and needs, too.

The majority of those in the study group tend to be persons who are in the midst of building their careers. A high percentage of them are in their 30's, 40's, and 50's. They report a higher level of formal education than those in any other group. As a group, they report an income that falls about midway between those who are in the fellowship group and the traditionalists.

Vocationally, those in the study group tend to be in management, supervisory, or professional positions. Many are self-employed. In rural areas, they are the farm owners or, perhaps, the owners and operators of small businesses. In an industrial center, they often hold management positions or are factory foremen or supervisors. A high percentage of those in educational and health care professions exhibit the characteristics of those in the study group. They tend to be persons whose daily occupation requires them to be mentally alert, to make decisions, and to study in order to keep abreast of changing conditions and circumstances.

Theological and Belief Patterns

Persons in the study group tend to hold to a well informed, moderate theological position which is only slightly to the left of center. They are very tolerant of those who may hold positions that are considerably different from their own. Instead of challenging those who hold different positions, persons in the study group often engage those with variant points of view in serious discussion because they are constantly looking for new insights and understandings.

Although those in the study group are very tolerant of other points of view, they have strong personal convictions and can usually articulate them clearly and well. They believe it is very important to develop and foster Christian attitudes that are consistent with their best biblical and theological understanding.

Because of this integrity, they have a strong social conscience, but they are not inclined to be crusaders or outspoken critics. They tend to live out their convictions rather than talk about them, unless circumstances call for stronger expressions. When those occasions arise, persons in the study group are usually capable of making their position known in a forceful and convincing manner. Sometimes they come on a bit too strong for others in the congregation who sometimes find it difficult to accept too many changes too rapidly.

Church and Sunday School Participation

Those in the study group believe strongly in the total mission of the church, including its ecumenical expressions. They are most supportive of the broadest scope of activities and programs, ranging from the very traditional to the latest forms of the church's ministry and work. When compared to the other audience groups, they are the least likely to withhold their money from the less popular causes that the church might choose to support.

Study group persons are very likely to be among those who represent their congregation in denominational as well as ecumenical events that are beyond their local community. A high percentage of those who attend and participate in denominational legislative bodies, as well as those who serve on boards and agencies that function beyond the local congregation, are from the study group.

Despite their heavy involvement in the ministry of the church beyond the local congregation, study group persons report the highest record of attendance in the Sunday school and the second highest record of attendance in the worship services of the local congregation.

They report a higher level of attendance and participation in the Sunday school, youth group, and worship services of their church during childhood and youth than those in any other group. In comparison to those from the other audience groups, a higher percentage of persons in the study group report that their parents, especially their fathers, took an active part in the life of the church when they were growing up. Prayer at meals was a common practice in most of their homes.

It is not uncommon for those in the study group to report that they dropped out of the church while they were preparing for their professional careers. This is especially true of those whose preparation required above average academic training. The drop out was usually not due to hostile feelings or to an anti-church attitude. Rather, these persons were so deeply engrossed in other things that the church was given a lower priority for a while.

If they were among those that dropped out temporarily, they are most likely to say that they returned because they, and perhaps members of their family, sensed a personal need for the faith that the church offered. They are also most apt to say that they want their children to receive quality Christian education.

Just as a high proportion of the study group members give time and leadership to the church beyond the local congregation, so also they tend to occupy key leadership positions in their local congregations. Many of them serve as teachers in the Sunday school, as counselors for the youth, and as sponsors or advisors for the college students. They are often chosen to serve as chairpersons of the official local church governing body, of the pastoral staff relations committee, or of the congregation's program planning and coordinating body.

Just as Ben Radcliffe was looking for a special kind of Sunday school class, so those in the study group want to be part of a class or small group in which they can engage in a serious study of the faith. They usually prefer a relatively small group in which they can engage one another in dialogue and discussion.

Study group persons want a teacher who serves more in the capacity of a study director. They prefer a teacher who does not have all the answers, but is a co-learner along with those in the class. Often when a class is made up largely of study group types, the members of the class take their turns teaching and leading the discussion.

Their curriculum preferences are in the direction of elective-type courses. The subjects of interest may range from rather sophisticated biblical studies to an examination of doctrinal and theological subjects, to a consideration of the role of a Christian in the workplace, or how to influence the outcome of a local community issue. They want their curriculum to be relevant and current. Thy tend to shy away from dated curriculum series.

While those in the study group are not anti-social, they do not place a great deal of emphasis on regularly scheduled social activities apart from the class periods. They may have one or two annual celebrations, but they do not usually feel the need for regular monthly class parties or other similar get-togethers. They tend to prefer the excitement and stimulus of a vigorous discussion to an evening of socializing.

What Are the Implications?

1. Study group persons usually can serve as "window openers" for the congregation. They can help create an awareness of the church beyond the local congregation and thus overcome the tendency for churches to become ingrown and provincial in function and outlook.

2. Study group persons are often influential in the

community and beyond. As such, they can extend the ministry of the church and the witness of the gospel into places that are often resistant to or suspicious of church sponsored efforts.

3. The distinct preferences of those in this group should be kept in mind when classes or groups are formed for persons with study group characteristics. They want an opportunity to name their teachers and leaders and to select their own curriculum resources. To fail to take those strong preferences into consideration could prompt some study group persons to look elsewhere for that which satisfies their perceived needs.

4. Those who are in the study group can be among the pastor's strongest allies. Their awareness of and commitment to the church—which extends beyond the local congregation—their openness to new learning, their leadership skills, and their tolerance for diversity of beliefs can enrich the ministry and extend the witness of every congregation.

5. There may be a tendency for those in the study group to become impatient when a class, a small group, or the church itself becomes overconcerned with the matters that they perceive to be irrelevant or of little importance.

6. Study group persons usually have the ability to serve effectively in organizational and leadership roles, but they should not be expected to show the same degree of enthusiasm when planning for the women's bazaar, fellowship activities of the church, or for the church's clothing drive.

7. Those in the study audience group do not usually identify their class with a particular classroom over a long period of time, but their classroom should be

equipped with good teaching aids—chalkboard or newsprint, reference materials, maps, and flexible seating arrangements.

8. While those in this group do not generally like dated curriculum materials, they do appreciate some continuity and do not like to interrupt that continuity in order to meet with other classes for joint or special class sessions.

9. If they should move and look for a new church home, the study group persons frequently do not select a church on the basis of denominational loyalty, but on the basis of what the particular congregation promises to offer. Once having made a commitment to a local congregation, they tend to be very interested in and committed to the denomination with which the local congregation is affiliated.

10. Because they are inclined to be well informed about the faith and tend to be very tolerant of those whose views may be different, persons from the study audience group frequently serve as very able teachers and leaders of classes that include those with a broad theological spectrum. They can appreciate the views of the neo-traditionalists as well as of those who are deeply interested in social action.

V

A Faith that Demands Action

It seems as if everyone in Central City knows Ruby Taylor, either in person or for her service to the community. Likewise, Ruby knows most of the city council members, the members of the school board and the voting commission, and those who serve on the planning commission.

An interest in the affairs of Central City have deep roots in Ruby's family. Her father was mayor when the voters adopted a city council plan for the growing county seat town. Her mother was one of the first women to serve on the school board. As Ruby was growing up, the family often talked about the growing pains that their town was experiencing as the population increased and several small industries were started.

When Ruby went away to college, she met John Taylor, who was studying to become a lawyer. They were married just after graduating from college. John enrolled in the state university to continue his training. Ruby got a job with the welfare department. As John was nearing the completion of his work at the university, Ruby's father told him about an opening in an old established law firm that had a long service record in Central City. John went in for an interview and was offered the position. After several years with that firm, John decided to run for the county district attorney's office. He was elected and served for twenty years in that office.

Ruby and John have three children. May and Sue are married and live with their families in other states. John, the youngest, is getting a degree in social work at the state university.

Through the years, Ruby has been actively involved with many issues and concerns that have arisen in Central City. Her activities have ranged from spearheading a voter registration campaign to extending the city waterlines out to an underprivileged area of the town. She has lost count of the causes she has championed in her constant effort to improve the quality of education offered through the local school system. After World War II, she helped plan for a community teen club, and more recently she has been lending her support to the senior citizens' center.

The church and her Christian faith have always been important to Ruby. During her youth, she was actively involved in the youth program and went to two work camps that her denomination sponsored in Appalachia. While in college she was active in the student movement and assisted in a tutoring program that the campus minister had organized.

When Ruby and John moved back to Central City, John transferred his church membership to First Church. They attended worship services fairly regularly; they joined a Sunday school class, and Ruby became quite interested in the work of the women's society. She was especially concerned about some of their special projects, both in the community and beyond; two issues that have claimed her lifelong support are hunger and world peace.

Last year, John died after a short illness. Since he had always been a strong supporter of Ruby in most of the causes she undertook, some people wondered if perhaps John's passing would cause Ruby to lessen her community activities. But Ruby says the church and her faith keep her batteries charged and help her discover even more important things to do. The church, to her, is a continual source of valuable information and provides her with opportunities for service, along with other like-minded persons. To go about doing good is Ruby's idea of the ultimate expression of her faith.

Mark and Jan Simmons moved to Metroplex City shortly after they were married, about five years ago. Mark is in his fifth year of coaching in an inner city high school. Jan, who is a registered nurse, works out of the health department as a visiting nurse.

Mark's dad could not understand why Mark decided not to accept a coaching position in a brand new suburban high school when it was offered to him last year. Mark explained the reasons behind his decision: "I feel that I am just beginning to win the confidence of the kids in our neighborhood. Right now they need someone who will stick with them and help them understand what education can do for them. Also, some of the kids are from broken homes, and they need an adult to whom they can relate and in whom they can trust."

Jan agreed with Mark, and added, "You know, I went into nursing because I thought it would offer a lot of job opportunities and steady employment. I did not realize until I took this job how important nursing care is to so many people. Most of my patients could not live at home if it were not for home nursing services. I have really become attached to some of my patients; they have almost become like family to me."

Mark and Jan are members of an old downtown church. The congregation is not as large as it once was. Sometimes they feel like they rattle around in the big old sanctuary with its beautiful, stained-glass windows. The members of the congregation are made up of a cross-section of Metroplex City. They are of several races, of different backgrounds, and include some of the wealthiest citizens as well as some who receive government assistance.

The energetic young pastor and his wife and the Simmons have become very close friends. They share a common concern for the people who live around them in the inner city. The four of them often get together in one of their homes for an evening of conversation and coffee.

Mark and Jan have helped organize a Sunday school class that does not follow a traditional curriculum outline; they use a number of elective courses and other resources. Their class is a very lively one. It seems that everyone gets into the discussions. Occasionally they have a guest speaker from the community who helps them grapple with a concern related to their neighborhood. Sometimes their discussions prompt them to develop a plan of action that may also require the assistance of others from the congregation or the community to help carry it out.

Mark and Jan both feel very strongly that their faith in Christ calls them to do those things that will help make their neighborhood a better place in which to live.

Personal Demographics

Ruby Taylor and the Simmons have the characteristics of the *social action group*. They believe strongly in causes and actions that will have an impact on the community and the world in which they live.

Persons of all ages are found in this group; however, the largest numbers are in two age groups: those who are forty-five or fifty and older and those who are in their twenties and thirties. This group has a higher percentage of women than any other group.

As a group, their formal education is second only to those persons in the study group. The older persons in the social action group report a relatively high income, while those who are in their twenties and thirties report incomes that are inclined to be about average or slightly below those of other young adults with equivalent education and training.

Vocationally, those in the social action group tend to favor people-centered and service oriented occupations. Those in the older age group are often married women or widows who are not gainfully employed outside the home. Many of them are married to husbands who have above average incomes, or they may have other sources of income that allow them to give many hours of service to various causes.

Those in the younger age group, like Mark and Jan, tend to choose careers that put them in daily contact with other persons. Often those with whom they work are the victims of circumstances or social conditions that stand in need of improvement.

Theological and Belief Patterns

Social action persons usually view themselves as being well toward the liberal end of the theological scale. A few of those in their twenties and thirties take a position that leans toward a conservative stance, but the majority feel that they are much more liberal than others in the congregation.

Along with this perception of others in the congregation, the social activists tend to become impatient with those who do not share their concerns. They often show a limited degree of tolerance for anyone whom they perceive to be unconcerned. This sometimes leads to strong differences of opinion and even open conflict.

In most instances, those in the social action audience group are inclined to place the pastor at about the same point on the theological scale as they place themselves. They do not always think alike, but because the pastor is usually viewed as someone attempting to bring about positive changes in the community and the world, this group tends to sense a kinship with him/her. They might espouse different causes, but many in the social action group often see the need to address several issues. And those in this audience group believe very strongly that the church should be an agent for social change.

The social activists are driven by strong convictions about those causes that claim their attention and to which they give themselves. They are often articulate and outspoken advocates for those changes they are trying to bring about. Because of their tendency to be rather aggressive, the social activists frequently generate hostility among those who want to conserve present values and traditions.

Some members of the social action group, like Ruby Taylor, are usually concerned about systematic conditions in their own community as well as world conditions. They tend to address issues through legislative and political systems. It is not unusual for them to be working on several causes at the same time. Each of these causes may affect totally different groups of people.

Others, like Jan and Mark, tend to become directly involved with a particular group of people close at hand. They are very likely to enter into the day to day experiences of those for whom they have a concern. They are persistent and are willing to make long-term commitments. Although they are interested in and concerned about state, national, and world concerns, they tend to focus most of their energies on the immediate problems and concerns that affect those persons with whom they live and work.

Those in the social action group are the least likely to maintain regular spiritual disciplines, such as daily Bible reading and prayers at mealtime. When compared to those in the other audience groups, a smaller percentage of the persons in this group say they have had a born again Christian experience. This does not mean that the Christian faith is unimportant to them. Their faith is often very important to them, and they are strongly driven to put their faith into action in the community and world in which they live.

Church and Sunday School Participation

Since they believe that the church should be an agent for social change, they give strong support to all those expressions of the church's ministry that they perceive to be making an impact on their community as well as on the world. Consequently, they are strong advocates of the National and World Councils of Churches, the United Nations, and other similar organizations.

Although many in the social action group have been members of their congregation for a long period of time, their long-term membership is often due to the fact that many in this group are older than those in the other groups. They do not attach a great deal of importance to denominational loyalty *per se.* Their loyalty is usually conditioned by the social witness of the congregation or denomination.

Persons in the social action group are very likely to have dropped out of the church once or twice. Their return has usually been prompted by the coming of a new pastor who emphasizes the role of the church in society, by a new awareness of the church's positive influence in the world, or, perhaps, by a deep seated conviction that God is at work in and through the church to bring about a better world.

Those in the social action group report the lowest record of attendance in church and Sunday school when they were children. Likewise, as adults, they have the lowest record of attendance in Sunday school and the poorest or next to the poorest record of attendance in the worship services of the church. Their irregular attendance is often due to deep personal involvement in some cause in the community or elsewhere. However, when the church, Sunday school class, or some group or organization in the church is addressing a cause in which these persons have a deep interest, they will be in attendance in order to learn more about the subject, to inform others about the issue, or to engage in some activity that is designed to bring about change and improvement.

Generally, persons in the social action group are not interested in most church organizations, especially those which deal with routine business matters. However, they are interested in and very supportive of those organizations and groups that make a strong social witness through their programs and activities.

The social activists do not usually feel the need for many organized social or fellowship activities, such as Sunday school class parties and congregational fellowship suppers. They are not anti-social; rather, their primary interests are elsewhere.

In terms of a Sunday school class, they place the highest value, among all the audience groups, on having a teacher who shows love and concern for all persons. They do not attach much importance to the teacher's knowledge of the Bible or beliefs of the church. They do expect their teacher, however, to have a strong social conscience and to be able to help them explore issues and what might be done about them.

Those in the social action group expect their curriculum resources to be current and relevant. They usually do not like a regular curriculum series, unless that series has a strong focus on the social dimensions of the gospel and faith. They prefer elective curriculum resources that address political, social, and economic issues which are of immediate concern and interest.

Some Implications

1. Social activists can be valuable resource persons in many areas of a congregation's ministry in the community and in the world. They are generally well

educated, are well informed about current issues, and are willing to give time and effort to those causes they think are important.

2. Since they are convinced that the church should be an agent for social change, activists are usually willing to represent the congregation in efforts to improve the community or to bring about various kinds of social reform.

3. If there are enough social action persons in a congregation to form a Sunday school class or small group for study and service, it is usually advisable to encourage them to do so, because they tend to be impatient with others, especially those who are of the traditional group.

4. Social action persons should not be expected to make long-term commitments to organizations and groups in which a social witness is subdued or missing. They are more comfortable working on short-term task forces that address one or two issues at a time.

5. For many social action persons, faith is a very private matter, and they do not like to be called on to lead just any Bible study, to lead in audible prayer, or to witness to their faith.

6. It is highly imperative that those who are selected to lead or teach a class or group that is largely made up of social action persons be able to demonstrate their love and concern for all persons and for those causes which have an impact on persons. Social activists are highly sensitive to personal need.

7. At times, social action persons may become so committed to a current idea that they may have little appreciation for traditions, history, or existing policies. They sometimes look on them as forces blocking those

changes they are attempting to bring about as soon as possible.

8. While the social activists generally have very little interest in ongoing organizations, they can and will serve very effectively as organizers of task forces or committees to launch a clothing drive, to gather food for the needy, to spearhead a drive to improve living conditions in a neighborhood, or to arrange for the adoption of a refugee family.

9. Those in this audience group can serve as excellent contacts to put the church in touch with persons in the community and the world who are well informed about ways to address community and world issues.

10. Persons in the social action group do not usually form strong attachments to a room or place of meeting. They are more interested in the kinds of resources and leadership that are available to challenge and inform them.

11. Social action persons can serve as excellent conduits for denominational social action emphases. Their basic interests and strong convictions prompt them to be well informed and eager to share the information with others in the congregation.

VI

The Glue that Every Congregation Needs

Marjorie and Ralph McKeen are the parents of two girls and one boy. Janice, at seventeen, is the oldest child, Mark is fifteen, and Betsy is ten going on sixteen. Ralph is a machinist in the local auto parts factory. Marj has a part-time job as a telephone operator. Janice works during the summer months as a lifeguard at the community swimming pool and after school in the winter months as a waitress in a pizza shop. Mark mows lawns for several neighbors in the summer months. And Betsy can hardly wait until she is old enough to go to junior high, where she wants to "try out for everything."

The McKeens have lived in Rapid Center most of their married life. In fact, Ralph grew up in a small nearby town and used to come to Rapid Center many times during his growing up years. Marj was from another city in the state. They met at a youth conference sponsored by the churches of their denomination.

The church had always been an important part of Ralph's life. For as long as anyone could remember, members of his family were among the key leaders in the small congregation in their community. From infancy, Ralph had attended Sunday school and the worship services. He made a commitment to Christ and joined the church while still in junior high. He was very active in the youth program of the church, both locally and in district and state activities.

Marj's parents did not go to church during her childhood. Her best friend, Marilyn, invited her to the youth conference when she was a junior in high school. Marj agreed to go because it sounded like fun. She was very impressed with the caliber of the other kids she met there, and, for the first time, she really learned to know some adults for whom the Christian faith was important. Of course, she always said that the best thing that ever happened was meeting and learning to know Ralph.

When Marj went home, she started going to Sunday school, the youth fellowship, and attended worship services occasionally. With the encouragement of Marilyn, some of the adults whom she learned to know in the church, and the pastor, Marj decided that she, too, wanted to become a Christian. She enrolled in the pastor's confirmation class, was baptized, and joined the church.

Marj and Ralph continued to see each other at church youth events and on other occasions. Eventually, they were married. When they were married, they decided that their home would be established on Christian foundations and the church would always be an important part of their life.

Through the years, they attended worship services in their church quite regularly. They saw to it that their children all received religious instruction at home as well as in the Sunday school. They also encouraged their children to attend church camp, and last summer Janice went to a work camp with a group of others from the congregation.

Ralph and Marj have belonged to several different Sunday school classes through the years, and they have enjoyed and appreciated every one of them. Ralph has served on several important boards and committees in the church, including the building committee when the new educational unit was being built. Marj took her turn teaching in the children's department of the Sunday school when Janice was in the fourth and fifth grades. Marj was also dean of the vacation Bible school for several years when Betsy was enrolled. Right now, Marj and Ralph are helping with the youth fellowship. Janice and Mark won't admit it, but they think their parents are really okay.

The McKeen's all love their church and almost everything about it. True to their membership vows, they support the church with their presence, their prayers, and their gifts. Their faith is very important to them, and they attempt to live according to their beliefs and the vows they made when joining the church.

Many of their closest friends are members of their church. They enjoy participating in a number of the activities in their church, because they provide opportunities to learn to know others and to keep in touch with one another.

Marj and Ralph have never quite understood why some persons in the church have become so agitated, through the years, over such things as curriculum resources that they did not like or a teacher who taught in an altogether different manner from the previous teacher or changes that a new pastor would introduce in the worship services.

When a few members of the congregation thought every one should join in a voter registration drive, others reacted very negatively because they felt that the church should stick to religion and not meddle in politics. Ralph and Marj helped calm things down. They had close friends on both sides and felt that each side had a right to it's point of view. Further, they did not think that those who held one view should attempt to force the others to see things their way. In their quiet, yet firm, manner they refused to take sides and helped those on each side understand and appreciate the others.

They were pleased, and a little surprised, when Pastor John made a special trip out to their home to thank them for their part in helping resolve what could have been a very disruptive incident. He told them that not only in this incident, but also on several other occasions he had observed that they had been the "salt of the congregation." Pastor John explained what he meant by calling their attention to Jesus' reference to salt in the Gospel of Matthew. The pastor told them that their response to the incident brought out the best in everyone.

Peter and Betty Kellogg have been married less than two years. It is the second marriage for both of them. Peter's first wife died after a long and painful bout with cancer. Betty divorced her first husband several years ago when she decided that she could not put up with his irresponsible behavior that was compounded by his drinking problem.

Peter has one daughter, who is enrolled as a senior in one of the Ivy League schools. Peter is a very popular and successful dentist. He came to Oak City upon completion of his training about twenty years ago. At first, he was associated with Dr. Osborne, an older dentist whose practice became larger than he could handle. Recently, Dr. Osborne retired, and Peter invited a younger dentist to become his associate.

Until his first wife became seriously ill, Peter and his family attended St. Mark's Church. He had been baptized and confirmed in a church of the same denomination years earlier. They were not deeply involved in St. Mark's, but enjoyed and appreciated the festive occasions, like Christmas and Easter. During his wife's long illness, the family could not attend the services, and Peter lost interest in the church.

Betty has two children. John is a senior in Oak City High and Cherry is a junior at the state university. Betty is an administrative secretary in the offices of the local Chamber of Commerce. She has worked there for almost fifteen years.

Betty and her two children had regularly attended and participated in an independent church that had started up in Oak City. But when Betty divorced her first husband, some of the older members of the congregation openly criticized her. She was hurt and did not feel comfortable in the congregation. One of her associates at work invited Betty to go with her to a Single Again Sunday school class at Grace Church. Betty hesitantly agreed to go with her friend one Sunday. Betty immediately felt accepted and met several other persons whom she had previously met in PTA or through business contacts.

John was happy in Grace Church, because several of the guys who played on the football team with him were in the youth fellowship. Cherry was relieved to know that her mother had found a church where there was a loving and caring group of persons who could help her through the post-divorce adjustment period. So, when Cherry came home for spring break, Betty and her two children transferred their church membership to Grace Church. They soon were deeply involved in a number of activities, in addition to the worship services, the Sunday school, and the youth fellowship.

Before Betty and Peter married, Betty raised the question about their future church relationship. Peter replied, "You know, I'm glad you asked. More recently I've noticed how important your church relationships are to you, and I've realized that something is missing in my life. I think that we should both belong to the same church."

Betty and Peter were married by Dr. Johnstone, the pastor of Grace Church. In a previous counseling session, he had stressed the importance of a shared faith and church relationship. When he learned that Betty and Peter had already discussed their future relationship to Grace Church, he arranged for the transfer of Peter's church membership to Grace Church.

Immediately after their marriage, Peter began attending the worship services with Betty, and they also joined a Sunday school class made up of other couples who were about their age. Peter was not surprised to learn that several of his patients were in the class.

The class was a new experience for Peter, but he soon became deeply interested in the discussions. Although the class was different from her Single Again class Betty appreciated the new realationships and the excellent teacher, who seemed to have an uncanny ability to involve almost everyone in exciting discussions centering around the contemporary meaning of the Christian faith in today's world.

Due to their different religious backgrounds, Betty and Peter sometimes found that they held different views, but it was a growing experience for them to try to understand each other.

When it came time for the election of new class officers, Peter and Betty were somewhat surprised that they were elected co-chairpersons. They saw this as a new challenge. Due largely to Betty's administrative skills, Peter's inquisitive and creative mind, and the new excitement they shared about the class, a surge of interest was shown by a number of the class members. What is even more important, several members of the class began to speak openly about their own growth in the Christian faith and life.

Multiple Interest Group

The McKeens, the Kelloggs, and Susan Radcliffe, whom we met in chapter 4, are typical of the large number of persons who have multiple interests. The *multiple interest group* is usually the largest audience group in most congregations.

Persons in the multiple interest group are those whose interests and characteristics include combinations of those found in two or more of the other audience groups. When the characteristics of persons in the multiple interest group are measured and compared with those found among the other audience groups, this group falls in the midpoint range of almost every characteristic. For example, those in this group perceive their theological position to be about halfway between that of those in the traditional group and those in the social action group. They are older than those in the study group, but younger than those in the traditional group.

Another significant finding concerning those in the multiple interest group is that well over half of these persons exhibit combinations of characteristics that include several of the dominant characteristics defining the fellowship group. Thus the profiles of the majority of those in this group consist of combinations of fellowship and study group characteristics or fellowship and traditional group characteristics or fellowship and social action characteristics. More often, they may have several dominant fellowship group characteristics and a dominant characteristic or two from two, or even three, of the other groups.

So, these findings suggest that those in the multiple interest group are likely to be somewhat normative of many congregations. In other words, they probably come close to being the typical, or average, members of the congregation. Now let's look at some of their characteristics.

Personal Demographics

Those in the multiple interest group usually include persons of all ages. In most congregations, they range in age from senior high students to senior citizens. Educationally, they tend to cluster toward the middle of the scale, although a few of them may be highly educated, while some may have received very limited formal training.

Those in the multiple interest group are likely to include persons who are employed in almost every occupation represented in the congregation. They tend to hold responsible positions in the work force. Many of them are employed as skilled laborers or craftsmen. Others are in the service occupations. A high percentage of persons who hold secretarial and clerical positions are found in the multiple interest group. A number of persons who are in one of the professional careers tend to exhibit multiple interest group characteristics. A high percentage of farmers and those associated with agriculture are also found among them.

Theological Position and Beliefs

The full range of theological beliefs may be found in the multiple interest group, but the average member of this group tends to perceive his or her theological position to be just a bit to the left of center and about midway between the traditionalists and the social activists. Like the Kelloggs, they may come from widely different religious backgrounds or, like Marj McKeen, from a home that was not related to any church.

However, like those in the fellowship group, they are not inclined to view others in the congregation as being either extremely liberal or extremely conservative. Nor do they attach a high level of significance to theological differences they may observe either within the congregation or in the pulpit. Like the McKeens, they tend not to be bothered by ideological or theological variations.

Their faith is usually important to most of them, but they are not inclined to take strong adversarial positions, such as would the traditionalists or, perhaps, the social activists. Most of the persons in the multiple interest group respect the views of others, and they, in turn, expect others to respect their point of view.

Church and Sunday School Participation

As might be expected, those in the multiple interest group maintain average records of attendance in the worship services and Sunday school. Some persons are very regular in attendance, while others are quite irregular.

In contrast to persons in the other four audience groups, those in the multiple interest group tend to be comfortable with a wide variety of curriculum resources, teaching styles, and ways of conducting the Sunday school class or other small group. They are also able to adjust easily and to accept changes in the worship services, such as those which may occur when there is a change of pastors.

Because of the tendency of persons in the multiple interest group to adapt readily to change, to tolerate differences, and to be comfortable with different styles of leadership and patterns of congregational and group participation, they are often the "glue" that holds congregations and groups together. For that reason, the role and presence of multiple interest persons is exceedingly important to the life and health of every congregation. They help maintain congregational and group equilibrium. They bring a balance to the life of the congregation and help facilitate, as well as control, the pace of change.

Implications

1. Since those in the multiple interest group have many of the dominant characteristics that are found in the fellowship group, and since the fellowship group is also the largest of the other four groups, it is obvious

that the most common expectation of laypersons centers around the need for significant interpersonal relationships. Those relationships not only help to attract persons to the church, but also are essential for assimilating new persons and for their continued growth and participation in the life of the congregation.

2. Those in the multiple interest group may be in transition from one group to another, or they may have an integrated concept of the Christian faith and life that includes some of the strongest characteristics of two or more of the audience groups.

3. Since a high percentage of those in this audience group have strong fellowship needs, they may want ample space and provisions for fellowship opportunities. They tend to look on the formal class periods as occasions for fellowship, and they also appreciate frequent social activities and class parties.

4. Their tolerance of diversity enables them to be comfortable with different teaching styles and a fairly wide range of curriculum resources. In fact, they often prefer variety in teaching styles and curriculum resources. Continuity may be maintained through those who serve as leaders or officers of a class or group.

5. Multiple interest classes often provide the setting for new class groupings to be formed. In some congregations, a primary function of multiple interest groups is that of helping persons to identify the style of teaching and type of curriculum resources they prefer. When several persons indicate a clear preference for one particular style of teaching or curriculum resource, this may be the signal that a new class or group is ready to spin off from the larger group or class.

6. Since persons with multiple interests are often the

"glue" that holds congregations together, they can usually be counted on to supply steady and dependable leadership for a number of groups, boards, and task forces in the congregation. Many of them have the ability to mold persons with widely divergent points of view into effective, cooperative units or groups.

7. Because many of those in the multiple interest group have come from a wide variety of religious backgrounds, they are often able to help persons from sharply different religious traditions make the transition into a new and sometimes bewildering tradition. This bridging function will become even more important in the future, with the increasing numbers of Roman Catholics and Protestants who are switching denominations.

VII

Real Differences

The Willing Workers' Sunday school class was organized about twenty-five years ago when a new educational unit was added onto the Mt. Zion Church. Bob and Sue Rogers, Mary Walton, Frank and Eva Byers, and several others were charter members of the class. They were all young adults then. Some of them had just returned from military service, others had moved to town to find a better job, but most of them had grown up in Apple City.

When they first organized the class, they decided that they wanted a strong emphasis on Bible teaching and asked their pastor to help them recruit a good teacher who knew the Bible. The pastor suggested they talk to Ed Mitchell, a real estate salesman, who was one of the leading laypersons of the congregation. They talked to Ed, and he agreed to teach them for a while. Except for about a year when Ed's wife was seriously ill, the Willing Workers have had no other teacher. They always appreciated his Bible expositions and were constantly amazed by the fresh insights he shared with the class.

One Sunday, Ed announced to the class that his eyesight was failing and he would have to give up teaching. Ed continued, "I've been thinking about it for a long time and did not want to tell you until I could suggest someone you might want as your teacher. I think I've found someone. I'd like to suggest that you think about asking George Barton to be your new teacher."

George Barton had come to Apple City to be the new speech and drama professor at the community college. He and his wife, Betty, had been attending another Sunday school class. In the class discussions, it soon became obvious that both George and Betty were excellent Bible students, and it was just a matter of time before someone would enlist them to teach.

When Bob Rogers, the class president, and Mary Walton, the class secretary, asked George about teaching the Willing Workers' class, he replied, "I'd really be glad to teach for a while, but I'd like to suggest that Betty and I serve as co-teachers." That sounded good to Bob and Mary, who reported their conversation with George to the class the next Sunday. The members of the Willing Workers' class were very pleased by the report. They agreed that someone should talk to the pastor and the Christian education committee chairperson about appointing George and Betty Barton to serve as the co-teachers of their class. Everyone thought that they would be excellent teachers for the class and approved of the appointment.

On their first Sunday, George thanked the class for inviting him and his wife to be their new teachers. He paid a most fitting tribute to Ed's long and much appreciated relationship with the class. Then he said, "You know that no one can ever teach exactly the way Ed did, and we know better than to try. But we believe that, as adults, we can learn in many different ways. So, we'll probably be doing some things in ways that are a bit different from what you have become used to. Our goal, just as Ed's was, is to discover what God is saying to us through the Bible."

The Willing Workers' class members liked what George said to them. But they were not quite prepared for the different ways in which George and Betty led the class. When George asked Frank Byers, who was a city councilman, what he thought Micah's message about justice had to say about enforcing the right-to-work laws, Frank was flabbergasted. The next Sunday, when Betty and George introduced a parable with a role playing exercise in which Apple City was the setting instead of a village on the shores of the Sea of Galilee, Sue Rogers felt that the Bartons had strayed too far from the original text. Then one Sunday, when Betty divided the class into six groups and suggested that each group move the chairs around to form a circle, that was a bit too much.

The Rogers and Mary Walton called on the Bartons in their home. Bob Rogers told George and Betty that the class members knew that the Bartons were good students of the Bible, and they knew that George and Betty, being educators, must be effective teachers. "But," he said, "we aren't used to all those different teaching methods, and that bothers us. Can't you just lecture to us like Ed did?"

What Was Happening Here?

The situation described above illustrates some of the different expectations that adults bring with them to their Sunday school class and other similar settings in the church. It is obvious that the dominant class characteristics of the Willing Workers are those of the traditionalists. Through the years, the members of the class have been totally unaware that a self-selection process has been operative. Week after week, their traditional expectations have been reinforced. When new persons joined the class, they accepted and became comfortable with the way in which the class and the teacher functioned. New members who were unable to adjust to the class patterns became inactive, dropped out, or went to another class that was more in keeping with their expectations.

George and Betty had been part of a class in which the dominant characteristics were those of the study audience group. That experience, coupled with their professional skills as educators, caused them to assume that the Willing Workers would probably appreciate some changes and would be challenged by and interested in different ways to study the Bible. But they underestimated the extent to which the Willing Workers had associated one teaching method with good Bible teaching.

By way of contrast, if Ed Mitchell, or someone else who taught by the lecture method, had been assigned to the Jolly Rogers' class, a different kind of reaction might have been expected. The Jolly Rogers' class was composed largely of persons whose characteristics were those of the fellowship group. Their rather casual manner of conducting the class, with open discussions in which all felt free to participate, would have been frustrating to Ed. Likewise, the members of the class would have difficulty understanding why Ed always felt he had to start on time and did not like to be interrupted because he felt he had to "cover the lesson."

Instead of talking with Ed or the pastor or the education committee chairperson about their frustrations and disappointment, many of the Jolly Rogers would simply stop attending the class and would most likely find other settings in which they could enjoy the fellowship of their friends. In some churches, similar circumstances probably contribute to the fellowship-types' low record of attendance in the public worship services and formal sessions of their Sunday school class. Their loyalty to the class or formal group is not usually strong enough to generate a confrontation with those who are in designated positions of leadership.

Real Differences

As we have noted in the previous chapters, persons in each audience group differ from those in another group in several ways. The differences are real and deeply rooted. In larger settings, there is room for diversity. But in the smaller settings, like those found in a Sunday school class, a Bible study or prayer group, a women's circle, or even in some of the administrative groups and organizations, the possibility of conflict is always present when persons from the different audience groups are brought together.

Those very honest and real differences among persons in many congregations are often most noticeable and easier to measure in Sunday school classes or other small groups that have been formed on the basis of age, sex, or marital status.

The figure below illustrates the amount of importance those in each of the five audience groups attach to selected qualities or characteristics of an ideal Sunday school teacher.

Figure I
QUALITIES OF TEACHERS VALUED
—BY AUDIENCE GROUPS—

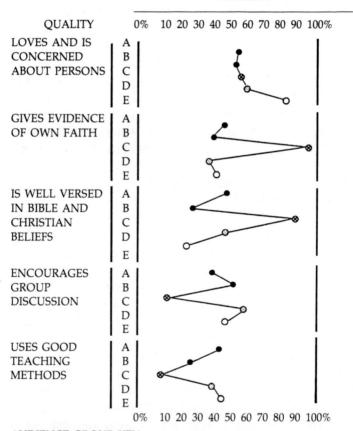

PERCENT

QUALITY   0%   10 20 30 40 50 60 70 80 90 100%

AUDIENCE GROUP KEY

A = MULTIPLE INTEREST   D = SERIOUS STUDY
B = FELLOWSHIP   E = SOCIAL ACTION
C = TRADITIONAL

*DIFFERENCES SIGNIFICANT AT P<0.01

Hartman, *A Study of the Church School in The United Methodist Church.*

Multiple Interest Group Expectations

Let's begin with the multiple interest group. Note that those in the multiple interest group tend to hold to the midpoint position in each of the teacher qualities, just as they do on most other profile characteristics. Some of the persons whose profiles show a strong traditional or a strong social action component may rate one or two of the values quite high, or they may place a low value on one or more of the characteristics. However, the overwhelming majority of those in the multiple interest group tend to take a moderate position. They apparently are not overly anxious or too disappointed when the teachers' characteristics or styles of teaching are not entirely in accordance with their expectations.

Fellowship Group Expectations

Those in the fellowship group attach considerable importance to ample opportunities for discussion. In fact, one can almost assume that if the teacher stimulates and encourages discussion among the class members and shows some love and concern for the members of the class, those who are in the fellowship group will be satisfied. They do not think that it is especially important for the teacher to be well-versed in the Bible or knowledgeable about Christian beliefs. Nor do many of them expect the teacher to use good teaching methods. Fewer than 40 percent of the fellowship group members think that it is important for the teacher to give evidence of his or her own personal faith.

As we noted earlier, their rather casual attitude about

the teachers' values relating to faith and beliefs also expresses itself in a rather indifferent attitude toward curriculum resources and other content-centered activities. They are primarily interested in those activities that foster interpersonal relationships and provide opportunities for stimulating interaction with others in the class.

Traditional Group Expectations

The figure on page 96 illustrates the very definite opinions and expectations of the traditionalists. They feel very strongly that their teacher must be one who gives strong evidence of his or her faith and is knowledgeable about the Bible and Christian beliefs. Since they place such a high premium on teachers who have a deep reservoir of superior biblical knowledge and theological understanding, and whose daily life is a living witness to a strong personal faith, the traditionalists tend to select their teachers with great care. Then, when they have a teacher who fulfills their high expectations, they strive to keep that teacher. It is not at all uncommon for traditional classes to retain the same teacher for years.

Just as they feel very strongly about what they want and value in a teacher, so also they feel strongly about those characteristics and values that are not important to them. They have virtually no interest in group discussions. In fact, many traditionalists deplore discussions, because the discussions tend to rob the teacher of time that they think he or she should spend in "teaching the lesson."

They also attach little importance to teaching methods. Many of them equate good teaching methods with group discussions and other activities that detract from the lecture.

Just as those in the fellowship group attach a high value to relational activities, so also the traditionalists place an even higher value on content-centered activities. Consequently, the selection of the proper curriculum resources is very important to them. They want curriculum resources on which the central emphasis is the Bible. Curriculum resources based on the outlines of the International Lesson Series are often found in traditionalist classes.

Study Group Expectations

Persons in the study group want a teacher who encourages and facilitates good group discussion. Most of those in the study group like to engage in stimulating discussion, and they attach more importance to group discussions than do those in any of the other four audience groups. Because most study group persons want ample opportunities to participate in group discussions, classes of no more than six or eight persons are common. If the class should become too large for all members to participate freely, some members of the class may pull out and start a new class.

They expect their teachers to love and to be concerned about all persons, to be moderately well informed about the Bible and Christian beliefs, and to be moderately skilled in their teaching methods. In all of these areas their expectations are about the same as those found among persons in the multiple interest group; they look at their teacher as a study director, as a discussion leader, and as a co-learner.

Study group persons attach less importance to the

teacher's witness to his or her own personal faith than do those in any other group. In the light of their deep commitment to the church and all of its ministries, the low expectation of their teacher as a witness seems a bit inconsistent. One explanation could be rooted in the fact that many in the study group are or have served, at one time or another, as teachers in the Sunday school. Also, it is a fairly common practice for those in study groups to pass teaching responsibilities around among themselves. Since many persons in the study group are teachers, they may be somewhat reluctant to say it is important for teachers to give evidence of their own personal faith in a winsome manner, lest it be implied that they think of themselves as exemplars of a winsome faith.

Curriculum interests and subject preferences of persons in the study group may range all the way from biblical archaeology to modern religious cults. Generally, these persons prefer fairly advanced elective curriculum resources. They are not usually interested in curriculum resources that they consider to be too elementary.

Expectations of the Social Action Group

Those in the social action audience believe that it is essential for their teacher to be one who loves and is concerned about all persons. Persons in the social action group attach more importance to this teacher quality than do those in any of the other four groups. This expectation is very consistent with the ongoing concern that those in this audience group have for persons and for those conditions that affect the quality of life.

They attach moderate importance to a teacher's ability to stimulate group discussion and to use different teaching methods. They do not attach much importance to the teacher's personal faith witness.

Only a few of those in the social action group feel their teacher should be knowledgeable about the Bible and of Christian beliefs. In fact, they attach less importance to this teacher characteristic than do those persons in any of the other four audience groups.

Accordingly, those in the social action group want curriculum resources that focus sharply on social and political issues. They expect the curriculum resources not only to be relevant, but also to be current and up-to-date. These persons are not inclined toward dated curriculum series, because they often feel that a series may lock them into a course of study that is apt to be outdated or would prevent them from addressing current issues as they arise. They prefer undated elective resources that can be supplemented with the latest current resources, such as the daily newspaper or weekly news magazines.

They do not expect their teacher to be unusually skilled as a discussion group leader, but they do expect him or her to be informed about social and political events, locally as well as nationally and internationally. Even more important, they want a teacher who believes in action and knows how and where to involve others in constructive activities.

Implications

1. The sharply divergent theological perspectives and the wide range of expectations concerning the ways classes should be conducted and taught suggest

that deliberate efforts should be made to offer several different options in every congregation, where space and leadership skills permit.

2. The above data call into question the traditional manner of forming classes and groups on the basis of age, gender, or marital status. Perhaps other criteria, such as classroom space, teaching style, subject matter, and group life expectations are more important factors and should also enter into the decision making process.

3. In the light of the very real differences that do exist among persons in the different audience groups, it may be advisable to actually disband and reform some classes and groups in order to eliminate the tensions and conflicts generated when persons from divergent audience groups are in the same class or group.

4. A wide variety of personal qualities and teaching styles, including lecture, is affirmed by the above data. Such consideration should be taken into account when teachers and leaders are paired with classes and groups.

5. Teachers and leaders would do well to remember that many times when members of a class or group express disappointment or dissatisfaction with a teacher, the criticism may not be due as much to the quality of teaching or leadership as it is to the style and manner of teaching and leading that is employed.

6. The above data clearly indicate that persons in several of the audience groups attend and participate in classes and groups not because they want to learn something, but because they want to be with others in an accepting and supporting group. Therefore, when those are the dominant expectations of a class or group, the sensitive teacher should encourage those kinds of

relationships and should not be overly concerned about "covering the lesson."

7. Since persons from the different audience groups tend to react in different ways to teaching styles and class procedures not to their liking, it is important for pastors and educational administrators to be on the alert for a variety of signs of dissatisfaction and discomfort.

8. When there are not enough persons or space to provide a class or group for each audience, it may be advisable to openly arrange for several different teaching styles and class procedures to be used occasionally.

9. Often, persons who are not related to any class or group in the congregation will become associated with a new class or group that is led by the pastor.

10. New classes or small groups can function as very effective ports of entry through which newcomers can make a comfortable entrance into the life of the congregation.

11. It is much easier to recruit persons for newly organized groups than for existing classes and groups that have a long history, a commonly accepted way of doing things, and have often unconsciously reached closure.

VIII

Getting off Dead Center

The Reverend Jim Moore has just moved to Berton to be the pastor of Hope Church. This is the second pastoral assignment for the personable thirty-two year old pastor. His first pastorate after seminary had been with two smaller rural congregations that were twenty miles apart.

Berton is a county seat town. Until very recently, the economy was very stable and the merchants and businesses of Berton flourished. The farm crisis was beginning to affect the economy, so everyone was delighted when it was announced that a large manufacturing company planned to build a small electronic components plant in Berton.

When Jim and his wife, Roberta, were contacted about the position by the personnel committee of Hope Church, they were quite excited. Raymond Masters, a leading businessman in Berton, was the chairman of the committee. He told Jim and Roberta about the new plant that would be starting operation in a few weeks and spoke glowingly about the boost the plant would be to Berton and to the whole county. Then he spoke of his hopes for the future of Hope Church. Looking directly at Jim, he said, "What we are looking for is a pastor with fresh ideas about how our church can reach out to the new families that will be moving to Berton."

Jim and Roberta gave serious thought to and prayed about the possibility of moving to Berton. Although they realized it would be difficult to leave the fine people in their two congregations, they decided that they would accept the new assignment if the personnel committee would extend an invitation to them. After several weeks, they received an official invitation from the committee, and they moved to Berton.

Jim was excited about the opportunity of serving a larger church in a county seat town. The move to Berton would also offer new opportunities for Roberta. She had worked as a visiting nurse in the largely rural area in which their other churches are located. She was a good nurse and had thoroughly appreciated the many opportunities for service that extended beyond the regular call of duty. She felt that was her ministry. Now she would have a chance to work in the new intensive care unit of the Berton Community Hospital.

Soon after Jim and Roberta arrived in Berton, Raymond Masters and his wife, Jane, invited them over to their home for an evening meal. After the dishes were cleared away, they all settled down in comfortable chairs in the den, and Raymond began to fill Jim and Roberta in on some of the history of Hope Church. He related some of the past achievements of the congregation and identified some of the fine citizens of the community who had been actively involved in the church's ministry within the community.

Then, after pausing a bit, his expression changed, and he said, "Would you believe that just after World War II our attendance boomed, and we had about three hundred in Sunday school and nearly four hundred in worship every Sunday? But for one reason or another, our attendance began to slip. I guess there were good reasons for it. Some of our young people went away to school and never returned; others were transferred to another town; some of our finest leaders died; and Berton changed. But I can tell you this, there are few churches anywhere that have played a more important role in the life of a community than Hope Church has through the years. Lately it seems that we are on dead center. Of course, we still have the old faithfuls who are here every Sunday. We don't have any trouble raising the budget. And our choir is as good as any choir in Berton. We have a good Sunday school and all the other necessary organizations. But when visitors come to our services, few of them come back. We try to make them feel welcome, but they end up going to some other church. We don't seem to be able to hold them."

During his first two months, Jim spent much of his time becoming acquainted with the members of Hope Church. Raymond Masters also saw to it that he met some of the most influential business and professional people of the community. Jim soon became aware of the fact that the Hope congregation was mainly made up of the old-line families in Berton. The problem of attracting new persons was not of recent origin, but had been one for several years. Apart from those who grew up in the families of the church or married into one of them, very few others had come into the church during the past ten years.

The church records showed that worship attendance was holding at about 225 persons every Sunday and had been for the last five years. When Jim asked Mrs. Apple, the church secretary, to fill him in on the organizations of the church, she replied: "Well, I guess that our children's division of the Sunday school is about average for a church our size. Of course, we don't have as many children as they have over in that new church on Oak Street, but we manage to hold our own. Most of the children of our church families attend our Sunday school. The same holds true for our youth. The young people who participate in Sunday school and in the youth fellowship are almost all from our church families who have been faithful members of Hope Church for years. Then there are the two adult Sunday school classes. One of them is taught by Miss Thompson. She is one of the best Bible scholars in all of Berton. Her lectures are never dull. That's why she has one of the largest Sunday school classes in town. The other adult class has two teachers who take turns teaching. One of them is Oscar Tucker, our mayor, and the other teacher is Marvin Masters, Raymond's son, who is in business with his father. People tell me that they really have some good discussions in that class. I guess that is the story about our Sunday school," Mrs. Apple concluded.

"Then," she continued, "the first Tuesday afternoon of every month the women of the church meet for their mission study. The men's club gets together for breakfast on the third Saturday of every month from October through May. They usually have a speaker who talks about some of the things related to our community. They don't meet during the summer months because they prefer to play golf, to go fishing, or to work in their gardens and yards on Saturdays."

Jim learned that the choir director was the music teacher at Berton High. He learned that Mabel Thornton, whose parents gave the organ to the church in memory of their own parents, had been the organist for the last fifteen years. Jim also noted that most of the choir members were in their forties and fifties. Someone told him that many of the choir members had been singing together since high school. Raymond was right; they were good.

During the first few weeks, Jim called on the new plant manager and his family when they moved to town. They came to Hope Church and soon joined. They really enjoyed the discussions in the Sunday school class taught by Oscar Tucker and Marvin Masters. Their son fit in quickly with the senior high Sunday school class and the youth fellowship.

Shortly before school began, the new high school coach and his family moved to Berton. The Tuckers brought them to Hope Church. Several new families with small children also moved to Berton to begin working in the new plant. Since Hope Church was of the same denomination as the churches from which they came, they also attended Hope Church when they first moved to Berton.

Despite Jim's and the Tuckers' best efforts and the words of welcome from Raymond Masters and several other members of the congregation, neither the coach and his family nor any of the other new families decided to make Hope Church their church home. Instead, they went to two of the other churches in Berton.

Out of utter frustration, Jim gave vent to the questions that had been building up inside himself and Roberta, but neither dared to voice them before: "Did we make a mistake when we came to Berton? Where did we go wrong? Is there any way to reach new people for Christ and Hope Church? Why can't we attract people like the coach and the other new families that are coming to town?"

What Was the Problem?

Let's not try to answer Jim's questions right now. Instead, let's try to see Hope Church from a different perspective.

In the preceding chapters, we have concentrated on persons who make up the five audience groups and the distinct profiles that are found in each group. We have discussed dominant personal characteristics, beliefs, attitudes, preferences, and expectations. We have also noted the ways of expressing faith and participating in the life of local congregations. Then, from those perspectives, we looked at Sunday school classes, small groups, fellowship activities and other congregational activities and organizations. In other words, we looked at congregations, and the organizations and groups within the congregations, through the lenses of those in each of the five audience groups.

Now, in this chapter we want to turn the lenses around and view the different audience groups from the perspective of the congregation. Specifically, how can an established congregation, like the one at Hope Church, examine its life in the light of what we know about the five audiences?

Without realizing what was happening, Hope Church became a congregation that ministered primarily to two of the audience groups—the traditionalists and those in the study group. Through the years, the other adult classes had died off. Now there were just the two adult Sunday school classes, the women's organization, the men's club, and the choir. All followed well-established ways of doing things, and they had become relatively self-contained groups.

Furthermore, each of them had reached their optimum sizes and closure had set in.

To be sure, everyone could enter into the worship services of the congregation. But Hope Church was an old established congregation, and most of the members had known one another for such a long time that some visitors tended to feel like outsiders. There were really no easy ports of entry, especially for those who were looking for fellowship relationships.

One Plan of Action

So, what can churches like Hope Church do to attract newcomers, as well as the unchurched who have always lived in the community? Before launching any plan of action, two very important points should be noted.

First, the existing ministry in most congregations is usually quite satisfactory to those persons who are now and have been a part of the life of the congregation. To use Hope Church as an example, the regularity of worship service attendance, the interest shown in the Sunday school and other organizations, and the support given to the financial needs of the church are all indicators of that satisfaction. Therefore, it is important to affirm those values that are present and, in most instances, not to disturb them.

Second, in most well established congregations there are many traditions that are strongly cherished. Consequently, innovations and changes come about slowly. Patience and time are essential ingredients of any plan of action to bring about new forms and expressions of ministry.

Any number of plans of action could be suggested

that might enable Hope Church to become more effective in its ministry within its community. Undoubtedly, no one plan will be totally effective, but here are some possible courses that can be taken:

1. Strive to discover what God would have the congregation be and do. This is the point of beginning. Almost every effective and growing congregation has a clear and commonly accepted understanding of the nature of its ministry.

Some congregations come to this understanding through prayer and Bible study. Others approach the question through a study of their community and the opportunities for service and ministry. Still others critically examine the ministry of their congregation and determine what the priorities should be in the future. Some name a long-range planning committee to draft a purpose statement, which is then studied and is used to serve as the basis for planning and ministry. Other congregations follow similar procedures or combinations of those listed above. The essential element is a common commitment to a commonly understood ministry.

2. Determine unmet needs and expectations. Many congregations that maintain the loyalty and devotion of a solid core of members are not aware of unspoken needs and expectations that may exist within the congregation as well as among others in the community.

Needs and expectations can be identified in a variety of ways. Neighborhood conversations, informal exploration groups, surveys and questionnaires, or the use of a belief and preference scale, similar to the one in the next chapter, can all be used to identify the different audiences, their preferences, and needs.

When the expectations have been clearly identified, the sensitive and wise pastor and congregational leaders will give serious attention to them. As we noted earlier, the expectations among different audiences are real and very important to those who hold them.

3. Set the thermostat on "friendly." Thousands of persons, both churched and unchurched, have been asked what they look for when choosing a church. Their replies show that by far the most frequently sought characteristic is the friendliness of the people in the congregation.

Some congregations that honestly believe they are friendly give the appearance of being quite unfriendly to newcomers and outsiders. Because the folks in some churches enjoy greeting one another and talking with their longtime friends, they often do not notice or take time to greet and talk with someone they do not know. No visitor likes to be ignored.

When several hundred persons in a national survey were asked to identify some of the reasons why they lost interest and dropped out, the largest number of them said that they did not feel needed or wanted. Broken or fractured relationships were the principal reasons they gave for losing interest and dropping out of the church.

An atmosphere, or climate, of warmth, friendliness, and caring does not just happen automatically. Deliberate and intentional planning and efforts on the part of a number of persons in the congregation are essential. The pastor can do much to set the climate in the public worship services, but, in the final analysis, those who are in the congregation and in all the other groups in the church, really determine the quality of relationships that persons experience and remember.

4. Organize new classes and groups. One of the surest ways of extending the ministry of every congregation is to form new classes and groups. Each should be designed to meet the needs and expectations of a particular group of persons. For example, the two adult Sundy school classes in Hope Church appealed especially to the traditionalists and to those in the study group. Furthermore, they had been together so long that for all practical purposes the classes were full, and it would have been exceedingly difficult for newcomers to break into the classes.

Little was being done to meet the needs of those in either the fellowship or the social action groups. The coach and his family, and some of the other young families who were new in Berton, were looking for a class or group that enjoyed being together and had a social life beyond the formal class sessions. They did not find that kind of group in Hope Church, so they went elsewhere.

Most of the mothers and wives who were employed outside the home could not attend the Tuesday afternoon mission study meetings of the women's organization. Some of them would probably be interested in some kind of group event that would meet during the evening hours. The focus of their concern might be on any one of several issues that would be of interest to them.

And the list could go on . . .

Research has repeatedly shown that whenever a new class or group is formed to expressly meet the needs and expectations of an identifiable group of persons, the average attendance in the total Sunday school increases by an amount equal to the average attendance of the new class. Furthermore, average attendance in the worship services of the church usually increases by an amount that is greater than the average attendance in the new class, because the new attendees often participate in worship services on a more regular basis, and they frequently bring other members of their family or their friends along with them.

5. Increase the number of service and participation opportunities. The limited number of organizational groups and programs in many churches tends to create a small elite group of persons who make most of the decisions, provide most of the formal leadership, and assume most of the responsibility for maintenance of the property. In many churches, like Hope Church, questions about who makes what decisions and who does what seldom arise. Those questions have already been answered. When this occurs, life in the church family is relatively calm on the surface and moves along with a minimum of conflict.

But, like Hope Church, many such congregations have unknowingly narrowed the scope of their ministry, have reduced their missional thrust, and are wondering where all the people went. Several significant studies have shown that church growth and an expanding ministry are directly correlated with the percentage of those persons in the church who are actively involved in some kind of service within, or on behalf of, the congregation. This is true for those who give formal leadership in designated or elected leadership positions, as well as for those who function in numerous informal ways.

In some of the most exciting and most rapidly growing congregations, efforts are made to involve every member in some avenue of service. Some pastors report that unless new members are related to a class or small group in which their expectations are fulfilled within sixty days after joining a church, those members are likely to become inactive within two years or less.

The above data should not be surprising to anyone. It is almost axiomatic that when we are given opportunities to contribute of our time, of our skills, and of our energy to any endeavor, we also claim ownership and feel we belong and are needed.

There is no easy way of moving a congregation off dead center. But a review of the basic task of the church—deliberately creating an open climate, providing new ports of entry through the formation of new classes and groups that are designed for specific audiences, and opening up opportunities for leadership and service—is one of the critical ingredients in the life of every church that would expand its ministry. Perhaps that is why the writer of the Acts of the Apostles attributed much of the vitality of the early church to teaching (and learning), to fellowship, to breaking bread, and to prayers. Everyone could participate in those acts of service and worship.

IX

How to Identify
Your Audience Groups

The five audience groups were first identified in a study that was completed in 1972. The profiles were quite sharply drawn in order to clearly establish the separate identity of each audience group. In the years that have followed, those basic profiles have been shared and tested with several thousand pastors, laypersons, Christian educators, professors, and church leaders.

Those with whom we have shared the profiles have repeatedly affirmed the presence of several, or of all, of the five audience groups in their own congregations. They have also helped flesh out the characteristics of those in each group, so that their "skeletons" were not quite so sharply defined. Very often, someone in a workshop or seminar will say, "We have every one of those audience groups in our church." Another will say, "Maybe one of our problems is that too many of our classes are alike, and we have catered to only one or two audience groups." Still others will offer the opinion that the majority of persons in their churches have always consisted of only one or two audience groups. And, occasionally, some will say that they feel that all of

116

their classes and groups are multiple interest groups.

It is highly unlikely that the composite profile of any given class or group will be 100 percent fellowship, traditional, study, or social action. Furthermore, we believe that each member of a class or group is a uniquely complex being who cannot be neatly pigeon-holed into one of the four audience groups. It is not our intention to do so.

Rather, our effort is in the opposite direction. We began with individual persons and attempted to identify and measure those characteristics which were unique to each person. We found, as might be expected, that a number of persons had certain characteristics in common.

We also found that when one or two characteristics were present in an individual or group profile, certain other clearly identified characteristics would also be found. For example, a high percentage of those who described themselves as being more conservative than others in the congregation almost always preferred a teacher who lectured and was well-versed in the Bible. And those who placed a premium on interpersonal relationships were not usually overly concerned about theological issues, but they did want enough unstructured time during the Sunday school hour to permit them to chat informally with a number of others in the class. It was often through those informal conversations that they ministered to one another more effectively than could either the teacher or pastor.

We also discovered that those in one audience group may hold in common certain characteristics that are found only in that audience group. Likewise, other audience groups have some other characteristics distinctively theirs.

The different sets of characteristics that are held in common by each audience group are deeply based, are very real, and, in their own way, are most important to each individual person. Such diversity does not necessarily create conflict, but the possibility of conflicts erupting is always present in almost every congregation and in every class or group in which there is such diversity.

Pastors and congregational leaders who are aware of the characteristics common to the different audience groups can provide those kinds of classes, groupings, and leadership styles that will not only do much to avoid conflict, but also will enhance relationships and will assist each person in his or her faith journey.

How Can the Audience Groups Be Identified?

As we have described the five audiences to pastors, Christian educators, and other church leaders, we have repeatedly been asked for an easy-to-use instrument that might identify the members of congregations by audience groups. The five audiences were originally identified by means of fairly sophisticated statistical analyses that required the use of a business or commercial computer. Since most pastors and local church leaders do not have ready access to such computer technology, we have developed an instrument that can be used in every local church to help determine the audience groups that are present in any particular class or in the congregation as a whole.

The instrument consists of thirty-two statements that are designed to identify and measure preferences and beliefs. Each statement is related to a dominant characteristic found in one of the four basic audience groups. An equal number of statements—eight—has been selected from each audience group profile.

We suggest that the statements be copied or duplicated in a format like that which appears below:

A Preference and Belief Profile

The following statements are designed to help your pastor and others know what you believe and what you prefer about your church, Sunday school class, or other small group in your church. There are no right or wrong answers. Please indicate your own personal agreement or disagreement with each statement.

SCORE

1. The church should stick to religion and not be concerned with other issues.   _____

2. I like plenty of time to visit with others in a class or group.   _____

3. Every class should have one or more community service projects.   _____

4. My beliefs are about the same as those held by most of those in my congregation.   _____

5. I like a teacher/minister who helps me think about several different interpretations of the gospel.   _____

6. I believe that one should hold some money back if he/she does not agree with the way the church is spending money.   _____

7. The quality of personal relationships that I have with others is more important to me than the teacher's style or the kind of curriculum resources we use.   _____

8. Most persons in our congregation are, theologically, more conservative than I am.   _____

9. I prefer a class/small group in which there are opportunities to discuss a wide variety of current concerns and issues. _____

10. My church should participate in interdenominational programs and events. _____

11. My church should do something about the social problems in our community. _____

12. I prefer a teacher or leader who lectures most of the time. _____

13. The congregation should give a high priority to denominational events and activities. _____

14. I prefer a Sunday school class/small group that has parties and other social activities throughout the year. _____

15. I expect my teacher to be well-versed in the Bible and the doctrines of the church. _____

16. I want to learn more about issues, such as international peace, justice, and human rights. _____

17. Most persons in our congregation are, theologically, more liberal than I am. _____

18. I want to develop Christian attitudes that are based on a clear understanding of the gospel. _____

19. The friendliness of the people in a church is more important to me than the kind of worship services they have. _____

20. The most important quality of a good teacher/leader is the ability to love and be concerned about all persons, regardless of their race or where they live. _____

21. I like a Sunday school class/small group that follows the same procedure every week. _____

22. I like a class/small group that is made up of people with the same interests, hobbies, and concerns that I have. _____

23. My church should give money to the United Nations and other peace-keeping efforts. _____

24. The most important task of a Sunday school class is to win others to Jesus Christ as Savior and Lord. _____

25. I prefer a teacher/leader who doesn't have all the answers but is a co-learner along with others in the class. _____

26. I prefer a class/small group that causes me to think about things I haven't considered before. _____

27. A teacher/leader should be well informed about social issues and have some ideas about what we should do about them. _____

28. The traditions and history of my church are very important to me. _____

29. I like to get together with other members of my class/small group just to have a good time. _____

30. We should take time to recognize personal things, such as birthdays, anniversaries, job changes, family, news, and so on. _____

31. Studies of community concerns and issues should be followed up with definite plans of action. _____

32. I welcome different opinions and ideas, because they help me develop a broader understanding of the Christian faith and life. _____

In order to properly administer the instrument, it will be necessary to make a copy of it for each person in the group or class that will be using the instrument. If you want to identify the individual respondents, members of a particular class or group, persons in certain age groups, or the gender of respondents, be sure to include space for that information. If you just want to have a rough idea of the makeup of persons in a class or group, or want to draw a large group or congregational profile, it will not be necessary to include any kind of identifiers on the instrument.

When you make copies of the preference and belief statements, it is a good idea also to prepare tally sheets. Make enough so that you will have one for each person who will be responding to the preference and belief statements. Across the top of each tally sheet, write the names of the four basic audience groups: Fellowship, Traditional, Study, and Social Action. Then in vertical columns under the audience group names write the eight numbers that are listed in each of the following columns. These numbers are assigned to the statements on the preference and belief sheet. Each number and statement is keyed to one of the four basic audience groups. For example, statement 1 refers to a characteristic that is associated with those in the traditional group. Statement 2 measures a characteristic that is dominant in the fellowship group, and so on. After each number, be sure to leave enough space to write in the score that the respondent has given to each statement. Your tally sheet should look something like this:

Tally Sheet

Fellowship	Traditional	Study	Social Action
2_____	1_____	5_____	3_____
4_____	6_____	9_____	8_____
7_____	12_____	10_____	11_____
14_____	15_____	13_____	16_____
19_____	17_____	18_____	20_____
22_____	21_____	25_____	23_____
29_____	24_____	26_____	27_____
30_____	28_____	32_____	31_____
Totals_____	_____	_____	_____

While you are preparing materials, you may also want to prepare separate answer sheets so that you can use the pages containing the thirty-two statements more than once. Very simple answer sheets can be prepared by listing the numbers from 1 to 32 on a separate page, or perhaps a 3″ × 5″ card. Be sure to leave enough space after each number for the respondent to write in his or her response.

Two Ways to Use the Instruments

There are two different ways the respondents may use the instruments. Before deciding which plan to use, you may want to test each plan on several persons. Now, let's look at the two plans:

Plan A. This is the easiest and fastest plan. Ask everyone to respond to each statement with a simple *yes* or *no* answer.

Plan B. This plan requires more work, but it is also more discriminating and gives more precise profiles. It calls for the use of a seven point scale:

Agree very much	+3	Disagree somewhat	−1
Agree	+2	Disagree	−2
Agree somewhat	+1	Disagree very much	−3
Cannot Say	0		

If you use Plan B, it is advisable to write the above scoring scale on newsprint or a chalkboard where all can see it; also include it at the top of the first page containing the thirty-two statements and on the answer sheets, if you use them.

It is important that all respondents in a group or class follow the same plan (the two plans will produce different scores). You should decide beforehand whether you will use Plan A or Plan B. Do not allow respondents to choose which plan they prefer; this will only generate confusion.

Administering and Scoring the Thirty-two Statement Instruments

When you are ready to administer the instruments, it is advisable to give the instructions to everyone in the classes or groups at the same time. Explain that the purpose of the instrument is to allow each person to indicate his or her preferences and beliefs about the church, the Sunday school, or any other group in order that those who are responsible for planning and administration might know everyone's individual needs and expectations. Since every statement is important, declare your hope that everyone will indicate his or her own agreement or disagreement with each of the thirty-two statements. Remind them that there are no right or wrong answers. This is not a test. This is simply one way to enable persons to identify their needs, their preferences, and their expectations.

Then distribute the thirty-two statement instruments. Give instructions about the scoring procedure you have decided to use, either Plan A or Plan B. Ask if there are any questions. Make sure that everyone has a pen or pencil. Allow plenty of time for everyone to mark his or her responses.

Computing the Scores

Under most circumstances, those who administer the instruments gather them and use the tally sheets to compute the scores. If you prefer to have the respondents tally and compute their own scores, give everyone a tally sheet and carefully instruct them how to use it.

If you used Plan A and asked for *yes* and *no* answers, give each *yes* answer a score value of + 1 and give each *no* answer a score value of 0. Use the tally sheets to record the score given to each of the thirty-two statements. If, for example, the respondent answered statement 5 with a *no*, then write 0 in the blank next to the number 5 on the tally sheet.

Then, add up the number of 1's in each of the four columns of eight numbers. The sums at the bottom of each of the four columns indicate the extent to which the respondent has identified with each of the four basic audience groups.

If you used Plan B, copy the exact score the respondent has given each of the thirty-two statements onto the tally sheet beside the number that corresponds to the statement number. Add up the positive scores in each audience group column; then subtract the negative scores from the positive total in each audience group column. This will give you four separate numbers, one at the bottom of each column. Those four numbers indicate the extent to which each participant does or does not identify with each of the four audience groups.

How to Interpret the Scores

When either of the two above processes has been completed, there should be four total scores—one for each audience group.

A high score in one audience group and low scores in the other three indicates that the respondent has preferences and beliefs that definitely place him or her in that one audience group. He or she would tend to be comfortable in a class or group that was designed especially for those in that particular audience group and would probably be, at best, only moderately satisfied with a class or group designed to meet the needs and interests of one or more other audience groups.

A high score in one audience group and a medium score in one or two audience groups indicates one primary interest and one or two secondary interests. Such a person would definitely prefer a class or group designed for the audience group receiving the highest score, but would most likely enter into the life of another class or group designed more along the lines of the secondary audience group.

A high score in two or more audience groups indicates that the person has multiple interests. This person would most likely be interested in most classes or groups and would tend to function quite well in them. He or she can usually adapt easily and readily to different styles of leadership and group procedures.

Low scores in all audience groups indicate little interest in classes and groups. This person may feel that his or her principal needs and interests are met adequately in congregational activities, such as worship services. Or low scores may reflect a disappointing or unpleasant experience in a class or group in the past.

Caution: Try to avoid putting people into pigeonholes or locking them into one or more of the audience groups. Our research is based on the probability that a group of persons tends to function and respond within a given range of behaviors. So, if a person's beliefs and preferences fit within the range of behaviors that have been used to identify one of the audience groups, we can say that there is a strong probability that he or she also holds a number of other characteristics in common with other persons who are in the same audience group. But at the same time, we must remember that while a person may hold many characteristics in common with others in the same audience group, everyone is a unique personality and may have some characteristics that are totally different from others in the group.

A second reason for caution is based on the fact that all of us are on a life journey. We noted earlier that many factors may prompt persons to move from one audience group to another when they are at different stages in their life and in their faith journey. Most of us discover that there have been times and events in our lives that have caused us to need and want entirely different relationships and experiences.

And Finally

We offer these thirty-two statements and these procedures not as firmly fixed and exact measurements. Rather, we consider them to be just one among many ways to determine some of the beliefs and preferences of persons found in most congregations, Sunday schools, and small groups.

It is our sincere hope and prayer that one or two ideas in the foregoing pages will contribute to your understanding of the ways that God works among us. To that end, we dedicate this book.